Do it yourself!

It doesn't necessarily take a highly trained service technician to make most repairs on an appliance. This book shows you just how easy it can be to repair your own range. Whether you're an avid do-it-yourselfer or just a beginner, the step-by-step photo instructions and detailed explanations will help you perform the majority of range repairs you're likely to encounter.

By learning to do as many of your own repairs as possible, you save time and money.

> **Safety information:** Electric ranges are complex electromechanical devices. Any attempt to repair your range may, if improperly performed, result in personal injury and property damage. General Electric Company cannot be responsible for the interpretation of this manual, nor can it assume any liability in connection with its use. For more detailed safety information see page 2 of this manual.

> **If your appliance is still under warranty:** Before you attempt any repairs, check to see if your appliance is covered under warranty. If you or any unauthorized service technician tries to repair an appliance under warranty, the warranty may be voided.

Step-By-Step Repair Manual for General Electric/Hotpoint Ranges
General Electric Co.

© 1985 by General Electric Co.
Appliance Park
Louisville, KY 40225

Contents

Note: Pages 1 through 8 contain important information. Be sure to carefully read these pages before you begin any repair procedures.

How to use this manual

General Electric Company has recognized the growing need for the homeowner to perform as many of the service operations as possible around the house. Consequently, we have prepared this manual to provide the typical homeowner with the information necessary to perform the majority of range repairs. This manual is written in an easy to follow, step-by-step, photo guide format to instruct you how to do your own repairs.

Before you begin your repair

It is important that before you begin any repair or diagnosis on your range you take the time to read the general information on pages 2 through 8. By acquiring a basic understanding of range repair and important safety information, you'll be a step ahead on diagnosing and remedying the problem.

Problem Diagnostic Charts

When a problem does occur, refer to the Problem Diagnostic Chart section of the manual (pages 8-15). These charts will help you pinpoint your trouble by listing possible causes from the most likely to the least common cause. The charts will refer you to the repair procedures (pages 16-89) that use photography and illustrations to show you step-by-step how to remedy the problem. Be sure to read the entire repair procedure carefully before attempting any work.

Glossary of Terms

If you find a term you don't understand, you may find it listed in the Glossary of Terms listed at the end of this manual (pages 101-103). Also, don't forget to use the index as a reference when searching for various information.

Read Your *Use and Care Book*

After you have read the introductory sections in this manual, you may want to re-read the *Use and Care Book* that accompanies your range. The *Use and Care Book* can tell you how to remedy many problems that aren't due to equipment faults, such as baking problems and clean-up procedures. You may just discover that your range has useful features you've forgotten.

Preventive Maintenance

When you have completed your repair, the Preventive Maintenance section (pages 91-93) can help you obtain the best results from your General Electric or Hotpoint range. Preventive maintenance is a vital key to long life for your range. The few minutes you invest in caring for your range properly can save you a great deal of time and trouble.

What repairs are covered?

Although the General Electric Company has introduced hundreds of range models through the years, similarities in basic components allow this manual to cover most common repairs. Some procedures may not apply to your range--for instance, your range doesn't have both pushbutton and rotary switches for the cooktop, but it will have one of the two.

Safety information

Electric ranges are complex electromechanical devices. Any attempt to repair your range may, if improperly performed, result in personal injury and property damage. General Electric Company cannot be responsible for the interpretation of this manual, nor can it assume any liability in connection with its use.

Safety precautions
To minimize the risk of personal injury or property damage it is important that the following safe servicing practices be observed:

---

1. **Be sure you are operating your range properly. Read carefully the *Use and Care Book* that comes with your range.**

2. **Know the location of your range's circuit breakers or fuses. Clearly mark all switches and fuses for quick reference. If you are unfamiliar with circuit breakers and fuses, please refer to Procedure #1: Power Supply, Circuit Breakers and Fuses.**

3. **Before servicing your range, turn all range controls OFF. Disconnect the power supply at the distribution panel by removing the fuse or switching off the circuit breaker. Unplug the range before inspecting, testing, or removing any access panel.** Note: **None of the repairs or tests in this manual require voltage to be applied to the range for testing.**

4. **When working with surface and oven units, be certain the units have cooled before trying to remove them from range.**

5. **Be careful when handling access panels, range parts or any components which may have sharp edges. Avoid placing your hand into any areas of the range which you cannot first visually inspect for sharp edges.**

6. **Never interfere with or by-pass the operation of any switch, component or feature of an electric range.**

7. **Use only replacement parts of the same size and capacity as the original part.**

8. **Before reconnecting the power supply, make sure no uninsulated wires or terminals are touching the cabinet. Electrical wiring and grounds must be correctly reconnected and secured away from sharp edges, high temperature, components and moving parts. All panels and covers should be reinstalled before the range is plugged in.**

9. **The internal wiring of electric ranges is made with special heat-resistant insulation. Therefore, ordinary wire should never be substituted. Since the wire carries heavy currents and is subjected to heat, it is especially important that all connections are tight and secure.**

10. **Carefully read through the entire repair procedure for a specific repair before attempting the job. If you don't fully understand the repair procedure or doubt your ability to complete it, call a factory service technician.**

11. **Throughout this manual additional safety precautions dealing with specific repair procedures will be presented. This information should be read carefully.**

12. **This manual does not apply to the repair or maintenance of any range with a microwave feature. Because of the high voltage and the critical nature of the door closure system for the microwave oven, do not attempt <u>any</u> repairs on these ranges. If you encounter problems with any range having a microwave feature, call a General Electric/Hotpoint service technician.**

Parts information

Obtaining replacement parts

If you're going to the time and trouble of repairing your appliance, it is important that you get the correct replacement part. First, be sure you have the complete model number for your appliance when ordering replacement parts. Even if you take in the original part, a salesperson may not be able to supply the correct replacement part without your complete model number. Second, to assure proper fit and performance, use Genuine General Electric Renewal Parts.

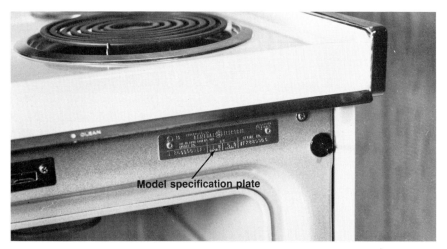

A common location for the specification plate that contains your range model number.

General Electric range specification plate

Hotpoint range specification plate

Finding your model number

The model and serial numbers of your range are stamped on a metal model specification plate. On free standing ranges and built-in ovens, you'll find this specification plate fastened to the oven frame. On built-in cooktops, the plate is riveted to the porcelain pan mounted underneath the cooktop. You can read it by raising the nearest surface unit and removing the reflector drip pan. On ceramic cooktop models, the specification plate is located on a label under the right front control knob.

The complete model number must be used when ordering exact replacement parts. Be sure to copy this number correctly and record it on page 90 of this manual for future reference.

Genuine GE Renewal Parts

All parts are not created equal when it comes to your General Electric or Hotpoint range. Some non-GE parts may require extra brackets and adaptors to make them fit. Others may not be designed for the exact electrical specifications of your range and, as a result, may cause substandard performance. With Genuine GE Renewal Parts you are assured a proper fit and performance match for the original part — an assurance that's backed in writing with a one-year limited warranty.

For your convenience in obtaining parts, General Electric has company-owned parts stores and authorized parts dealers throughout the country. To find the outlet nearest you, look in the Yellow Pages under major headings, "Appliances-Household-Major" or "Ranges & Ovens," then subheads, "Service & Repair" or "Supplies & Parts." If you are unable to find where GE parts are sold in your area, call The GE Answer Center™ consumer information service toll free 800-626-2000 for assistance.

Some dealers feature the Quick Fix® system of GE common re-

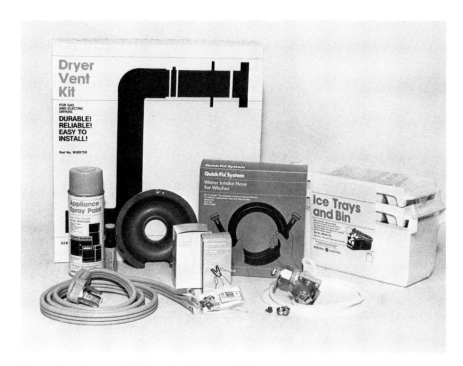

Genuine General Electric Renewal Parts are backed by a one-year limited warranty to assure you proper fit and performance.

placement parts and parts kits. Designed specifically for do-it-yourselfers, Quick-Fix® parts come in clearly marked packages complete with hardware and step-by-step replacement instructions.

Whether it's the Quick Fix® system or the regular GE line of parts, you should insist on the performance and quality of Genuine General Electric Renewal Parts. After all, if you're investing time and money to care for your appliance, it's better to do it right the first time and not chance problems later from using an unsuitable part.

How your electric range operates

This section provides background information about how an electric range operates. Because the more you know about the operation of your range, the easier it will be for you to understand the causes and solutions for a range problem.

What exactly happens when you turn your range on? Electricity from the household circuit is delivered to a terminal block inside your range through three large wires inside the power cord. Electrical power is then distributed through a network of internal wiring to the various range components (shown in the drawing on the right). Basically, there are two types of components-- heating units and heating unit controls.

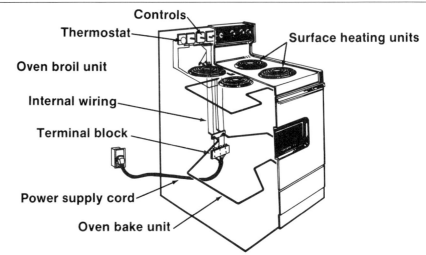

Controls
Thermostat
Oven broil unit
Internal wiring
Terminal block
Power supply cord
Oven bake unit
Surface heating units

Heating units

The heating units are insulated metal coils that are wound to supply a certain electrical resistance and reach certain temperatures. Oven units are shaped to provide an efficient heating area for the oven size and airflow. While the bake and broil units may look similar, they have different design specifications and cannot be interchanged.

The Calrod® cooktop surface unit was developed by General Electric. Inside the durable external steel sheath is a nichrome coil that is surrounded with an insulating compound. Some Calrod® surface units may have one or more coils, depending on the cir-

cuitry and type of control system. Ceramic cooktops have surface units hidden beneath a smooth, glass-like material.

Heating unit controls

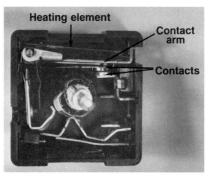

Heating element
Contact arm
Contacts

Heating units are controlled by a variety of switches and thermostats. Switches are used to turn the surface and oven heating units on and off; thermostats provide the correct amount of power to maintain the selected heat level in the heating units.

One type of switching method for range cooktop surface units is called an infinite-heat switch, so named because an infinite number of heat levels can be obtained between the high and low positions. Inside the switch is a tiny electric current heating element and a contact arm made from two dissimilar metals bonded together. As the electric current heats this arm, the unequal expansion rates of

the metals cause the arm to bend or warp. This bending moves the arm to open the switch contacts. As the arm cools, it bends back and allows the contacts to close and reheat the element. The result is a "pulse" of power cycles reaching the element.

A second kind of surface unit switch is found on some ranges with either pushbutton or rotary-type switches. These switches combine various arrangements of circuits and voltages to provide distinct heating levels and are called fixed-heat switches.

A common type of an oven thermostat control mechanism is a sealed capillary tube. The tube contains a heat-sensitive material that expands when the heat increases (breaking the contacts that energize the heating unit) and contracts as the oven cools (allowing the contacts to touch and re-energize the unit).

Self-clean controls

To reach the high temperatures needed to clean an oven and also protect the homeowner from these high temperatures, there are additional control systems used in self-clean ranges. This manual covers two of them--the solid-state control system, and a more recent dual range thermostat control system. It's important to know which self-clean system you have before attempting to diagnose or repair oven malfunctions. Open your oven door and look inside at the top left of the rear wall. The pictures below will help you identify which system is present in your self-clean range.

Solid-state control system

The solid-state system is comprised of several control components. A printed circuit board controls the oven temperatures through a sensor resistor (the protrusion on the inner oven wall in the side picture). This sensing control is powered on a separate circuit by an oven transformer. A hot wire relay cycles the heating units on and off during the clean cycle, while the high temperature limit switch locks the door in the clean cycle and guards against excessive temperatures during baking.

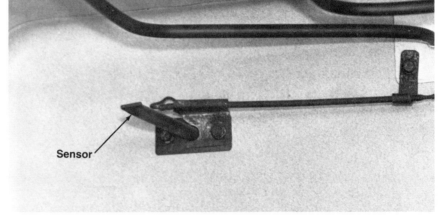

You can tell if you have a solid-state control system two ways--1) there is a protrusion on the top left of the inner rear wall that has a flat-shaped tip; and 2) the oven temperature control knob has mechanical "stops" at the WARM and BROIL settings.

Dual range thermostat control system

In the dual range thermostat oven, the thermostat controls both normal cooking and cleaning operations. It is used with a thermal switch safety device (the protrusion on the inner oven wall in the side picture) that locks the door in the clean cycle and keeps the heating units from overheating during normal operation.

Note: If your oven looks different from either of these pictures, it likely features a sophisticated electronic self-clean control system that should be repaired only by a service technician.

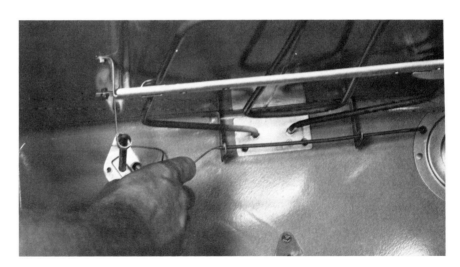

You can tell if you have a dual range thermostat control system three ways--1) there is a rod-like protrusion on the top left of the inner rear wall that is supported not only at the rear wall but also by a bracket coming down from the top of the oven; 2) the capillary tube under the broil unit on the rear wall is supported in two brackets; and 3) the oven temperature control knob has a pointer on the CLEAN setting and "snaps" when rotated clockwise into the CLEAN position.

Models covered

Over the years, General Electric and Hotpoint have produced hundreds of various range models in several different configurations. Repairs on most models are similar, so most problems that may arise with your range are likely to be covered in this manual.

Free Standing range is designed as a free standing unit although it is often installed between cabinets. Controls are on backsplash.

Built-in range is designed to fit a standard 27″ range cabinet and generally features up-front controls and an optional backsplash.

Hi/Low range is a complete cooking center with the convenience of two ovens. It has eye-level controls and ceramic or Calrod® surface unit cooktop.

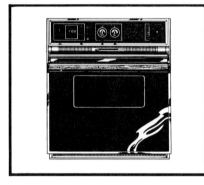

Slide-in range is a versatile range that is designed to slide into a 30″ opening between cabinets, but can also be used as a free standing unit.

Built-in oven is usually used with a separate built-in cooktop for a custom kitchen look. Single or double ovens feature eye-level controls.

Built-in cooktop features ceramic glass, or Calrod® surface units possibly combined with a grill/griddle. Controls are on cooktop or range hood.

Exceptions

This manual does not include any repairs for gas ranges, microwave ovens, or ranges with a microwave feature. It also does not cover repairs for electronic touch control mechanisms, but will apply for some standard component repairs on the "touch control" ranges.

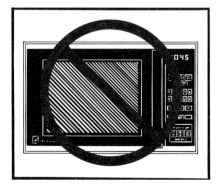

Problem diagnostic charts

How to use the problem diagnostic charts

The problem diagnostic charts help you with one of the most difficult tasks in do-it-yourself repairs...locating the possible causes and solutions to your problem. Before using the charts, make note of the problem you are experiencing with your range. Keen observation can often lead you to the area where the problem lies. Watch for anything that deviates from normal operation. Note everything that is or is not working. Once you have identified a problem, then you can begin to solve it by referring to the Problem Diagnostic Charts.

The Problem Diagnostic Charts are divided into three sections: problems that occur with all range models; problems that apply only to self-cleaning ranges with a solid-state control system; and problems that relate to self-cleaning ranges with a dual range thermostat control system. To determine which control system your self-cleaning range uses, see page 6.

The Problem Diagnostic Charts are divided into four columns of information: (1) **Problem**; (2) **Possible Cause**; (3) **Repair Procedure**; and (4) **Skill Level**. The first column, **PROBLEM**, lists examples of problems you may encounter with your range. In the second column, there is a list of **POSSIBLE CAUSES** that may be the reason for the problem. The possible causes for each problem are listed in the order in which they might be expected to occur, from the most likely to the least likely. A **REPAIR PROCEDURE** for each possible cause is listed in column three. Repair procedure information refers you to a course of action to remedy the possible cause of your range problem.

The final column, **SKILL LEVEL**, indicates a skill level rating for each repair task. This rating will help you decide which repairs you feel confident of completing.

●	Easy	No previous experience needed
● ●	Average	Requires removal of service panels. Mechanical ability is helpful.
● ● ●	Difficult	May require the use of an ohmmeter and/or splicing of electrical wires. Repair or replacement of component parts is more difficult.
● ● ● ●	Very difficult	Requires the use of an ohmmeter and the ability to read a circuit diagram. Repair or replacement of component parts is complex.
● ● ● ● ●	Requires Service Technician	Requires special tools and skills

No matter what skill level assigned to a task, study the repair procedure and safety instructions carefully before proceeding.

NOTE: The problems listed below are numbered exactly as they appear in the PROBLEM column of the Problem Diagnostic Charts.

I. All range models

1. Range does not heat (lights, timer do not operate)
2. Range does not heat (some lights and timers may not operate)
3. All surface units heat on low position only (fixed-heat type surface units only)
4. All surface units inoperative (oven operates)
5. Individual surface unit does not heat (single-coil plug-in type)
6. Individual surface unit "full on" high heat at all positions (single-coil plug-in type)
7. Individual surface unit does not heat (one-coil wired type)
8. Individual surface unit does not heat (two-coil wired type)
9. Surface unit partially heats (two-coil wired type with fixed-heat type switch)
10. Surface unit partially heats (three-coil wired type)
11. Automatic (Sensi-Temp™) surface unit temperature setting incorrect
12. Automatic (Sensi-Temp™) surface unit does not heat
13. Heat leaking around oven door
14. Oven temperature incorrect (oven not baking properly)
15. Bake unit does not heat (broil unit operates)
16. Broil unit does not heat (bake unit operates)
17. Oven won't work on timed bake
18. Clock timer does not operate
19. Appliance receptacles inoperative (range heats)
20. Timed appliance receptacle inoperative (lights and other receptacles operate)
21. Oven light does not work
22. Damaged range body
23. Oven door glass dirty or broken

II. Self-clean solid-state control system

24. Oven does not heat on bake, broil, or clean cycle (surface units operate)
25. Oven heat does not come on until control knob turned up
26. Incomplete cleaning
27. Oven does not clean (bake and broil cycles operate)
28. Bake and broil units do not heat (clean cycle operates)
29. Oven door does not release after cleaning

III. Self-clean dual range thermostat control system

30. Oven does not heat on bake, broil, or clean cycle (surface units operate)
31. Incomplete cleaning
32. Oven does not clean (bake and broil cycles operate)
33. Bake and broil units do not heat (clean cycle operates)
34. Oven door does not release after cleaning

Problem diagnostic charts

I. ALL RANGE MODELS

Problem	Possible Cause	Repair Procedure	Skill Level
1. Range does not heat (lights, timer do not operate)	No power to range (house fuse blown)	Check Power Supply (See p.17 & Procedure #1)	•
	Open wire between terminal block and range component	Check Wiring and Connections (See p.25 & Procedure #5)	•••
	Terminal block inoperative	Check Terminal Block (See p.23 & Procedure #4)	••
	Power cord defective	Check Power Cord (See p.19 & Procedure #2)	•••
2. Range does not heat (some lights and timers may not operate)	Fuse blown	Check Power Supply (See p.17 & Procedure #1)	•
	One conductor open between terminal block and switches	Check Terminal Block (See p.23 & Procedure #4)	••
	Poor connection on one side of terminal block	Check Wiring and Connections (See p.25 & Procedure #5)	•••
	One of three conductors in power cord open	Check Power Cord (See p.19 & Procedure #2)	•••
3. All surface units heat on low position only (fixed-heat type surface units only)	Range not receiving full power (range or house fuse blown)	Check Power Supply (See p.17 & Procedure #1)	•
	Open wire between terminal block and range component	Check Wiring and Connections (See p.25 & Procedure #5)	•••
	One of three conductors in power cord open	Check Power Cord (See p.19 & Procedure #2)	•••
4. All surface units inoperative (oven operates)	Open wire between terminal block and switches	Check Wiring and Connections (See p.25 & Procedure #5)	•••
5. Individual surface unit does not heat (single-coil plug-in type)	Open wire to unit	Check Surface Unit (See p.27 & Procedure #6)	••
		Check Wiring and Connections (See p.25 & Procedure #5)	•••
	Poor connection at surface unit receptacle	Check Surface Unit Receptacles (See p.29 & Procedure #7)	••
	Open surface unit	Check Surface Unit (See p.27 & Procedure #6)	••
	Open infinite-heat switch	Check Switch (See p.39 & Procedure #12)	••

Skill Level Index: • Easy •• Average ••• Difficult •••• Very Difficult ••••• Requires Service Technician

6. Individual surface unit "full on" high heat at all positions (single-coil plug-in type)	Infinite-heat switch defective	Replace Switch (See p.39 & Procedure #12)	••
7. Individual surface unit does not heat (one-coil wired type)	Poor connection at surface unit terminal	Check Surface Unit (See p.31 & Procedure #8)	•••
		Check Wiring and Connections (See p.25 & Procedure #5)	•••
	Open surface unit	Check Surface Unit (See p.31 & Procedure #8)	•••
	Open infinite-heat switch	Check Switch (See p.39 & Procedure #12)	••
8. Individual surface unit does not heat (two-coil wired type)	Poor connection at surface unit receptacle	Check Surface Unit (See p.33 & Procedure #9)	•••
		Check Wiring and Connections (See p.25 & Procedure #5)	•••
	Open surface unit	Check Surface Unit (See p.33 & Procedure #9)	•••
	Open fixed-heat switch	Check Switch (See p.37 & Procedure #11)	••••
9. Surface unit partially heats (two-coil wired type with fixed-heat type switch)	Poor connection at unit terminal	Check Surface Unit (See p.33 & Procedure #9)	•••
		Check Wiring and Connections (See p.25 & Procedure #5)	•••
	One coil open in surface unit	Check Surface Unit (See p.33 & Procedure #9)	•••
	Bad connection at fixed-heat surface unit switch	Check Switch (See p.37 & Procedure #11)	••••
	Open fixed-heat switch	Check Switch (See p.37 & Procedure #11)	••••
10. Surface unit partially heats (three-coil wired type)	Poor connection at surface unit terminal	Check Surface Unit (See p.35 & Procedure #10)	•••
		Check Wiring and Connections (See p.25 & Procedure #5)	•••
	One coil open in surface unit	Check Surface Unit (See p.35 & Procedure #10)	•••
	Poor connection at coil size selector switch	Check Switch (See p.41 & Procedure #13)	••
	Open coil size selector switch	Check Switch (See p.41 & Procedure #13)	••
11. Automatic (Sensi-Temp™) surface unit temperature setting incorrect	Improper calibration	Check Surface Unit (See p.43 & Procedure #14)	•••

Skill Level Index: • **Easy** •• **Average** ••• **Difficult** •••• **Very Difficult** ••••• **Requires Service Technician**

Problem diagnostic charts

Problem	Possible Cause	Repair Procedure	Skill Level
12. **Automatic (Sensi-Temp™) surface unit does not heat**	Open sensor	Check Sensor (See p.43 & Procedure #14)	•••
	Poor connection at unit terminal	Check Surface Unit (See p.43 & Procedure #14)	•••
		Check Wiring and Connections (See p.25 & Procedure #5)	•••
	Open wire between responder and unit	Check Responder (See p.43 & Procedure #14)	•••
		Check Wiring and Connections (See p.25 & Procedure #5)	•••
	Open surface unit	Check Surface Unit (See p.43 & Procedure #14)	•••
	Open responder	Check Responder (See p.43 & Procedure #14)	•••
	Open transformer	Check Transformer (See p.43 & Procedure #14)	•••
13. **Heat leaking around oven door**	Door not aligned properly with range body	Adjust Oven Door (See p.46 & Procedure #16)	•
	Oven door gasket damaged	Check Oven Door Gasket (See p.49 & Procedure #18)	•••
	Oven door hinge assembly damaged	Check Oven Door Hinge (See p.53 & Procedure #19)	•••
	Oven door spring broken	Check Oven Door Hinge (See p.53 & Procedure #19)	•••
14. **Oven bake temperature incorrect (oven not baking properly)**	Thermostat not calibrated properly	Adjust Oven Thermostat (See p.64 & Procedure #24)	••
	Open bake or broil unit	Check Units (See p.57 & Procedure #20)	••
		(See p.59 & Procedure #21)	•••
	Broken wire between oven selector switch and thermostat	Check Switch (See p.61 & Procedure #22)	••••
	Open oven selector switch	Check Switch (See p.61 & Procedure #22)	••••
	Oven door not adjusted properly	Adjust Oven Door (See p.46 & Procedure #16)	•
	Oven door gasket damaged	Check Oven Door Gasket (See p.49 & Procedure #18)	•••
	Oven door hinge broken	Check Oven Door Hinge (See p.53 & Procedure #19)	•••
	Oven vent blocked	Check Oven Vent (See p.45 & Procedure #15)	•

Skill Level Index: • Easy •• Average ••• Difficult •••• Very Difficult ••••• Requires Service Technician

15. Bake unit does not heat (broil unit operates)	Open bake unit	Check Bake Unit (See p.57 & Procedure #20)	••
	Open wire between bake unit and thermostat	Check Bake Unit (See p.57 & Procedure #20)	••
		Check Thermostat (See p.65 & Procedure #25)	•••
		Check Wiring and Connections (See p.25 & Procedure #5)	•••
	Open oven selector switch	Check Switch (See p.61 & Procedure #22)	••••
16. Broil unit does not heat (bake unit operates)	Open broil unit	Check Broil Unit (See p.59 & Procedure #21)	•••
	Open wire between broil unit and oven selector switch	Check Broil Unit (See p.59 & Procedure #21)	•••
		Check Switch (See p.61 & Procedure #22)	••••
		Check Wiring and Connections (See p.25 & Procedure #5)	•••
	Open oven selector switch	Check Switch (See p.61 & Procedure #22)	••••
17. Oven won't work on time bake	Controls not properly set	See *Use and Care Book*	
18. Clock timer does not operate	Range fuse blown (some models)	Check Fuse in Range (See p.73 & Procedure #28)	•
	Foreign object has clock mechanism jammed or worn mechanism	Check Clock Timer (See p.67 & Procedure #26)	•••
	Clock timer defective	Replace Clock Timer (See p.67 & Procedure #26)	•••
19. Appliance receptacle inoperative (range heats)	Range fuse blown	Check Fuse In Range (See p.73 & Procedure #28)	•
	Open wire between fuse and appliance receptacle	Check Range Fuse and Appliance Receptacle (See p.73 & Procedure #28)	••
		Check Wiring and Connections (See p.25 & Procedure #5)	•••
	Receptacle defective	Check Appliance Receptacle (See p.73 & Procedure #28)	••
20. Timed appliance receptacle inoperative (lights and other receptacles operate)	Clock timer defective	Replace Clock Timer (See p.67 & Procedure #26)	•••

Skill Level Index: • Easy •• Average ••• Difficult •••• Very Difficult ••••• Requires Service Technician

Problem diagnostic charts

Problem	Possible Cause	Repair Procedure	Skill Level
21. Oven light does not work	Light burned out	Check Light (See p.69 & Procedure #27)	•
	Open light switch	Check Switch (See p.69 & Procedure #27)	•••
	Oven light socket defective	Check Socket (See p.69 & Procedure #27)	•••
		Check Wiring and Connections (See p.25 & Procedure #5)	•••
22. Damaged range body	Scratches and dents	Check Range Body Cosmetics (See p.63 & Procedure #23)	•
23. Oven door glass dirty or broken	Inner glass surface dirty or broken	Check Oven Door Glass (See p. 47 & Procedure #17)	•••

II. SELF-CLEANING OVEN SOLID-STATE CONTROL SYSTEM

(See p.6 to identify your type of self-clean oven)

Problem	Possible Cause	Repair Procedure	Skill Level
24. Oven does not heat on bake, broil, or clean cycle (surface units operate)	Open oven sensor	Check Oven Sensor (See p.75 & Procedure #29)	•••
	Open hot wire relay	Check Relay (See p.83 & Procedure #33)	•••
	Open wire or poor connection at oven selector switch	Check Switch (See p.61 & Procedure #22)	••••
		Check Wiring and Connections (See p.25 & Procedure #5)	•••
	Oven temperature control inoperative	Check Oven Temperature Control (See p.81 & Procedure #32)	•••
	Open oven transformer	Check Transformer (See p.77 & Procedure #30)	••••
	Open oven selector switch	Check Switch (See p.61 & Procedure #22)	••••
	Open smoke eliminator	CALL SERVICE TECHNICIAN	•••••

Skill Level Index: •Easy ••Average •••Difficult ••••Very Difficult •••••Requires Service Technician

25.	Oven heat does not come on until control turned up	Solid-state control malfunction	CALL SERVICE TECHNICIAN	● ● ● ● ●
26.	Incomplete cleaning	Controls not set properly or clean time too short	See *Use and Care Book*	
		Bake unit not heating	Check Bake Unit (See p.57 & Procedure #20)	● ●
		Broil unit not heating	Check Broil Unit (See p.59 & Procedure #21)	● ● ●
		Oven door not sealing properly	Check Oven Door Gasket (See p.49 & Procedure #18)	● ● ●
		Improper cleaning calibration	Check Solid-State Oven Temperature Control (Printed Circuit Board) (See p.81 & Procedure #32)	● ● ●
27.	Oven does not clean (bake and broil cycles operate)	Range fuse blown (some models)	Check Fuse in Range (See p.74 & Procedure #28)	●
		Controls not set properly	See *Use and Care Book*	
		Clock timer defective	Replace Clock Timer (See p.67 & Procedure #26)	● ● ●
		Open oven selector switch	Check Switch (See p.61 & Procedure #22)	● ● ● ●
		Solid-state oven temperature control (printed circuit board) defective	Replace Printed Circuit Board (See p.81 & Procedure #32)	● ● ●
		Door latch mechanism inoperative	CALL SERVICE TECHNICIAN	● ● ● ● ●
		Open smoke eliminator	CALL SERVICE TECHNICIAN	● ● ● ● ●
28.	Bake and broil units do not heat (clean cycle operates)	High temperature limit switch defective	Replace Switch (see p.79 & Procedure #31)	● ● ● ●
		Door latch mechanism inoperative	CALL SERVICE TECHNICIAN	● ● ● ● ●
29.	Oven door does not release after cleaning	Oven not cool	See *Use and Care Book*	
		Door latch mechanism inoperative	CALL SERVICE TECHNICIAN	● ● ● ● ●

Skill Level Index: ● Easy ● ● Average ● ● ● Difficult ● ● ● ● Very Difficult ● ● ● ● ● Requires Service Technician

Problem diagnostic charts

III. SELF-CLEANING OVEN
DUAL RANGE THERMOSTAT CONTROL SYSTEM

(See p.6 to identify your type of self-clean oven)

Problem	Possible Cause	Repair Procedure	Skill Level
30. Oven does not heat on bake, broil, or clean cycle (surface units operate)	Open wire or poor connection at oven selector switch	Check Switch (See p.61 & Procedure #22)	••••
		Check Wiring and Connections (See p.25 & Procedure #5)	•••
	Open oven selector switch	Check Switch (See p.61 & Procedure #22)	••••
31. Incomplete cleaning	Controls not set properly or clean time too short	See *Use and Care Book*	
	Bake unit not heating	Check Bake Unit (See p.57 & Procedure #20)	••
	Broil unit not heating	Check Broil Unit (See p.59 & Procedure #21)	•••
	Oven door not sealing properly	Check Oven Door Gasket (See p.49 & Procedure #18)	•••
32. Oven does not clean (bake and broil cycles operate)	Controls not set properly	See *Use and Care Book*	
	Dual range thermostat defective	Check Dual Range Thermostat (See p.87 & Procedure #35)	••••
	Clock timer defective	Replace Clock Timer (See p.67 & Procedure #26)	•••
	Open smoke eliminator	CALL SERVICE TECHNICIAN	•••••
	Door latch mechanism inoperative	CALL SERVICE TECHNICIAN	•••••
33. Bake and broil units do not heat (clean cycle operates)	Open thermal switch	Check Thermal Switch (See p.85 & Procedure #34)	••••
	Door latch mechanism inoperative	CALL SERVICE TECHNICIAN	•••••
34. Oven door does not release after cleaning	Oven not cool	See *Use and Care Book*	
	Open thermal switch	Check Thermal Switch (See p.85 & Procedure #34)	••••
	Door latch mechanism inoperative	CALL SERVICE TECHNICIAN	•••••

Skill Level Index: • **Easy** •• **Average** ••• **Difficult** •••• **Very Difficult** ••••• **Requires Service Technician**

Repair procedures

How to use the repair procedures

The following range repair procedures take you step-by-step through repairs for most of the range problems you are likely to encounter. The Problem Diagnostic Charts on pages 8-15 will help you to pinpoint the likely causes of your problem. Beginning with the most likely cause, you can then refer to the appropriate repair procedure section. Like the Problem Diagnostic Charts, the Repair Procedures are divided into three categories: repairs that apply to all model ranges, repairs for self-cleaning oven ranges with solid-state control systems, and repairs for self-cleaning ovens with dual range thermostat control systems. See page 6 to determine which control system your self-cleaning range uses.

Each repair procedure is a complete inspection and repair process for a single range component, containing the information you need to test a component that may be faulty and to replace it, if necessary. This format breaks down even some of the most complex repair problems into separate, easy-to-handle units. Following the instructions given, you can test each component separately, isolating the cause of the problem and replacing any faulty parts. If one procedure fails to locate the failed component, you simply refer back to the Problem Diagnostic Charts for the next most likely cause of the problem.

Featuring a close-up photograph of the component you will be testing, the repair procedure begins with a description of what the component does and how it works. In the case of a component which varies with different range models, you will be shown how to determine which type is found on your range.

Instructions showing how to test and replace the component begin with steps that must be followed to assure your safety. Other initial steps indicate the skills and equipment that will be needed for the task. If you are uncertain about a process that will be used, such as reading a circuit diagram, using an ohmmeter, or removing access panels, you are referred to the pages in this manual where that process is discussed in detail. No matter what your skill level, careful attention must be paid to these instructions and safety precautions before you begin any procedure.

Clear photographs of typical range models illustrate each step of every repair procedure, proceeding from visual inspection and testing to replacement of the component. Because of the diversity of range models available, your range may differ somewhat from the illustrated model. However, each procedure has been carefully designed to be representative of the entire General Electric and Hotpoint lines, and as much information as possible has been included to help you make repairs on most General Electric and Hotpoint ranges.

NOTE:
The repair procedures are listed below in the order in which they appear in this section. Refer to the Problem Diagnostic Charts on pages 8-15 for the procedure most likely to remedy your problem, then use this list to locate the desired procedure.

All range models

1. Circuit Breakers and Fuses
2. Power Cord
3. Access and Control Panels
4. Terminal Block
5. Wiring and Connections
6. Surface Units: Single-coil plug-in type
7. Surface Unit Receptacles
8. Surface Units: One-coil wired type
9. Surface Units: Two-coil wired type
10. Surface Units: Three-coil wired type
11. Fixed-Heat Surface Unit Switch
12. Infinite-Heat Surface Unit Switch
13. Surface Unit Coil Size Selector Switch
14. Automatic Sensi-Temp™ Surface Unit
15. Oven Vent
16. Oven Door Adjustment
17. Oven Door Glass
18. Oven Gaskets
19. Oven Door Hinges
20. Oven Bake Unit
21. Oven Broil Unit
22. Oven Selector Switch
23. Range Body Cosmetics
24. Oven Thermostat Adjustment
25. Oven Thermostat (non-self-cleaning)
26. Clock Timer
27. Range Lights
28. Appliance Receptacles

Self-cleaning oven with solid-state control system

29. Self-cleaning Oven Sensor
30. Self-cleaning Oven Transformer
31. High Temperature Limit Switch
32. Solid-State Oven Temperature Control
33. Self-cleaning Oven Hot Wire Relay

Self-cleaning oven with dual range thermostat control system

34. Thermal Switch
35. Dual Range Thermostat

1 Inspecting circuit breakers and fuses

Skill Level Rating:	Easy	Average	Difficult	Very Difficult

Electricity produced by the power company is delivered to your house through a series of connecting power lines. A power supply distribution panel is located at the point where the main line from the power company enters your home. One of two types of distribution panels services your household, i.e., a circuit breaker panel or a fuse panel. From the distribution panel the power line is divided into a number of smaller circuits which are distributed to various household appliances, receptacles, and lights. Each of these circuits is protected from becoming overloaded by either a circuit breaker or fuse.

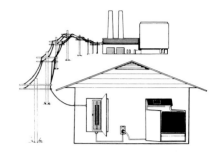

Circuit breaker type panel

Fuse type panel

It's important to know which breakers or fuses protect each circuit in your home. It's also wise to label them when everything is operating correctly, so you'll know which breaker or fuse to look for in time of trouble.

The distribution panel is the place to turn off all power on the range circuit before unplugging and servicing it. And it's the first place to look when problems occur. A tripped circuit breaker or blown fuse is a minor problem, but it can stop the entire range from working. **Note:** There are two circuit breakers or fuses controlling the power to your range. If you are unable to identify the location of these double circuit breakers or fuses, contact a qualified electrician.

Step 1: Be sure all range controls are turned **OFF**. Avoid touching any grounded objects such as water pipes when working around power supply. Stand on a dry insulated surface such as a dry board.

Step 2: This procedure requires the use of an ohmmeter. For instructions on how to use an ohmmeter, please refer to Tools and Testing Equipment, page 96.

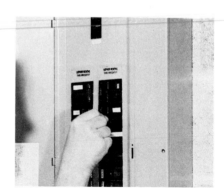

Step 3: Other than opening the door to the distribution panel, never remove any cover or expose any electrical terminals.

1 continued

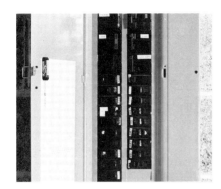

Step 4: Circuit breakers. Circuit breaker distribution panels contain rows of switches. When a breaker "trips", power is shut off and the breaker switch moves to an intermediate position between the "ON" and "OFF" points.

Step 5: To restore power, turn the breaker switch to "OFF" position, then back to "ON". If the breaker trips again, the circuit is still overloaded. Further exploration of the problem must be remedied before power supply can be restored.

Step 6: Fuses. A second type of distribution panel is protected by fuses. The large fuses used for a range circuit are contained in a fuse block. The small glassfront fuses are for smaller receptacle circuits.

Step 7: Range fuse blocks have a separate circuit to which nothing else is attached. A double-pole fuse block (two cartridge type fuses joined together at the handle) protect this circuit.

Step 8: Range fuses are accessible by pulling block out of panel, which also disconnects the range. A sharp forward tug releases block.

Step 9: Range fuses can be checked with ohmmeter. Set meter to lowest resistance scale, then touch probes to brass caps at each end of fuse. If no continuity, replace with fuse no larger than that specified by manufacturer.

Step 10: When reinstalling fuse blocks, "ON" notation should appear at top of block. Be sure fuses clip firmly in place. Loose connections can cause fuse to overheat.

2 Inspecting and replacing power cord

Skill Level Rating:	Easy	Average	**Difficult**	Very Difficult

Because of the heavy current necessary to operate ranges, the range power cord has much larger wires and plug than ordinary appliance cords. In the case of built-in and some free-standing ranges, power cords are not needed since cable is connected directly to the range.

If the range fails to operate properly, the power cord may be preventing power from reaching the range. Most problems of the power cord are caused by damaged and loose connections and will likely be visible.

Note: All built-in and some free-standing ranges do not have power cords because they are directly wired to the power distribution panel. If your range is directly wired, take extra precautions to be sure range's circuit breakers or fuses have been disconnected.

Range power cord

Step 1: Be sure all range controls are turned **OFF**. Disconnect the power supply at the distribution panel. Watch for sharp edges.

Step 2: This procedure requires the use of an ohmmeter. For instructions on how to use an ohmmeter, please refer to Tools and Testing Equipment, page 96.

Step 3: Protect floor cover and pull range away from wall to make power cord visible between range and receptacle. Inspect cord for visible damage.

2 continued

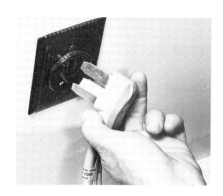

Step 4: Pull plug from receptacle with a firm, quick tug. Always grasp by plug and never by cord. Be careful not to contact blades of plug.

Step 5: Inspect plug carefully for damaged, corroded or burned terminals. Look carefully around molded portion for signs of overheating. If plug is damaged, replace cord.

Step 6: Remove rear access panels. If you are unfamiliar with this process, please refer to Procedure #3: Removing Access and Control Panels.

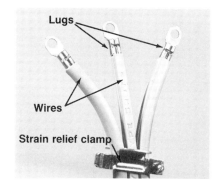

Step 7: Visually inspect power cord connection at terminal block. Inspect wires, lugs, and strain relief clamp. If any of these parts are damaged, replace power cord.

Step 8: If no visible damage is detected, an ohmmeter must be used to check for defective wires in the power cord.

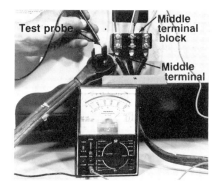

Step 9: To test cord, set ohmmeter to R x 1 scale. Clamp one test probe to terminal block. Middle terminal on block should always indicate continuity to middle terminal on plug.

Step 10: Outer terminal on block should indicate continuity to one but not both of the outer terminals on the plug. With meter probes in place, twist cord to be sure no internal break occurs. Replace cord if needle drops.

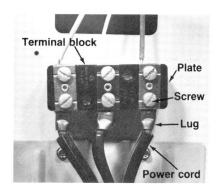

Step 11: To remove power cord unscrew the three screws that retain lugs between plates on terminal block.

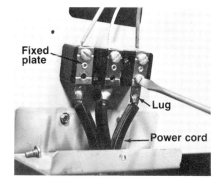

Step 12: When installing new power cord, connections at terminal block should be secure. Lugs of power cord go under fixed plate beneath screw.

3 Removing access and control panels

Skill Level Rating:	Easy	Average	Difficult	Very Difficult

For reasons of safety and appearance, all electrical and mechanical components of a range are enclosed. Many repairs require the removal of access panels in order to reach the parts.

All wiring and electrical connections at the rear of the range are covered by sheet metal panels attached to the cabinet with screws. Most repair jobs can be carried out when the rear service panel is removed. On some models, some repairs may require removal of a front panel to reach the components.

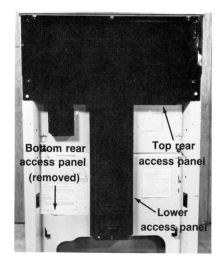

Bottom rear access panel (removed)

Top rear access panel

Lower access panel

Step 1: Be sure all range controls are turned **OFF**. Disconnect the power supply at the distribution panel and unplug the range from the receptacle. Watch for sharp edges.

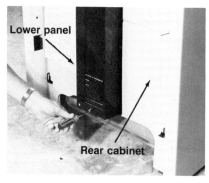

Lower panel

Rear cabinet

Step 2: Removing lower panels. Starting at the bottom, remove the screws that retain the lower panel to the rear cabinet. When removing the last screw, support the panel so it doesn't fall to the floor.

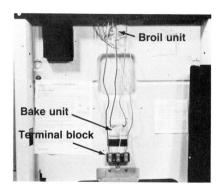

Broil unit

Bake unit

Terminal block

Step 3: Removing the lower panel exposes broil element wiring, bake element wiring and terminal block.

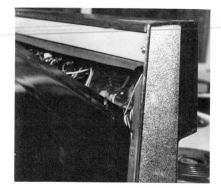

Step 4: Removing upper panels. Upper panels can be removed by loosening screws at top of panel. Pulling panel away will expose switches and wiring underneath.

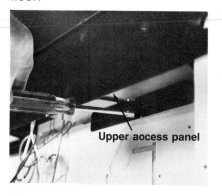

Upper access panel

Step 5: Look for screws in locations where the panel turns under to fasten to cabinet. Also, look for screws along cabinet edges. Note type of screw used in each location.

Latch pin (older models)

Latch pin (newer models)

Step 6: Removing range hoods: To gain access to switches on ranges with attached hood, release latch pin under flip out section of hood. (On current models latch pin is part of lip at edge).

3 continued

Step 7: With hood out of the way, upper retaining screws can be removed. If panel has a screw rather than hinge at bottom, provide support when hood is removed.

Step 8: With retaining screws out, control panel may be pulled slightly forward or hinged downward for access to switches. (Do not remove green grounding wire. Panel can be pulled as far out as necessary with caution.)

Step 9: Control panel on eye-level oven of some high-low ranges hinge downward for access to controls. Capillary tubes from thermostats are covered with insulating tubing to prevent contact with live terminals. Note terminal block mounted to left wall.

Step 10: Wall ovens. These ranges are designed to allow servicing from the front without removing range from wall or cabinet. To remove service panel, locate and unscrew screws.

Step 11: With retaining panel lowered on wall oven, wiring, switches and timer are exposed. Heating units can be removed from inside oven. Pull out top oven rack to support extended control panel.

Step 12: Built-in ranges. Switch panel on most built-in ranges and cooktops can be removed after first removing retaining screws. After screws are unscrewed, move panel upward to release from spring clip.

Step 13: With switch panel loose, switches, pilot lights,wiring harness and timer are accessible. Switches can be freed from panel by removing mounting screws located under knobs.

Step 14: Built-in and drop-in ranges with controls mounted on backsplash can be serviced from front. Remove retaining screws at each side of end cap to release backsplash.

Step 15: With screws removed, entire backsplash assembly can be pulled forward and lowered. Remove access panel to reach controls and wiring.

4 Inspecting and replacing terminal block

Skill Level Rating: | Easy | **Average** | Difficult | Very Difficult |

The power cord is connected to the range at the power supply terminal block. From the terminal block, internal wiring carries the power to the various circuits of the range.

Most problems at the terminal block are caused by loose connections and are usually visible in the form of either burned and oxidized terminals or damaged insulating material.

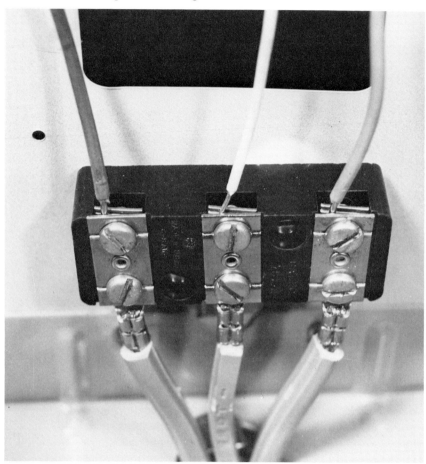

Terminal block

4 continued

Step 1: Be sure all range controls are turned **OFF**. Disconnect the power supply at the distribution panel and unplug the range from the receptacle. Watch for sharp edges.

Step 2: Remove lower access panel. If you are unfamiliar with this process, please refer to Procedure #3: Removing Access and Control Panels.

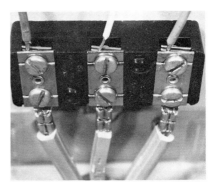

Step 3: Visually inspect terminal block for burnt terminal connections. If damaged, replace with new terminal block.

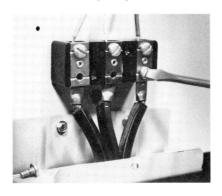

Step 4: To replace terminal block, first remove power cord. Cord is removed by unscrewing the three screws that retain lugs on terminal block.

Step 5: Next, loosen the upper three screws and pull internal wiring free. Terminal block can be released from the cabinet by removing two screws recessed into insulation material of block.

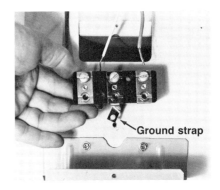

Step 6: Removing screw from ground strap attached to middle terminal allows block to be completely removed. Since this strap grounds range cabinet, be sure to replace it after new block is installed.

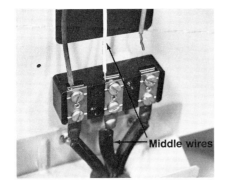

Step 7: To install new terminal block, reattach ground strap to the range cabinet. Connect middle wire of power cord and white wire of internal wiring to middle terminal of block. Be sure all wires and lugs are secure.

Step 8: Some four conductor terminal blocks are found on ranges installed in mobile homes and apartment complexes. These ranges have a four conductor power cord without a ground strap.

5 Repairing wiring and connections

Skill Level Rating: | **Easy** | **Average** | **Difficult** | **Very Difficult** |

Power is carried to the components of the range by a network of specially insulated heat-resistant wire. These wires are connected to switches and range heating units by various types of terminals. Some wires are mounted under screws, while others attach to a terminal that's part of the component.

It's very important that the wiring is free from damage. Any cut that reduces the diameter of the wire reduces the amount of power it will carry. A damaged wire will cause a component to receive insufficient voltage for proper operation. Also, the wire itself may overheat and eventually break at that point.

Wires connected to terminals are very susceptible to damage because of arcing and heat build up. If damaged terminals appear to be bright and shiny, they can usually be repaired. If they become dull and oxidized from excessive heat, they should be replaced. Any mating terminal, such as one located on a heating unit or switch, should be polished until bright and shiny before a new wire is attached to insure a good connection.

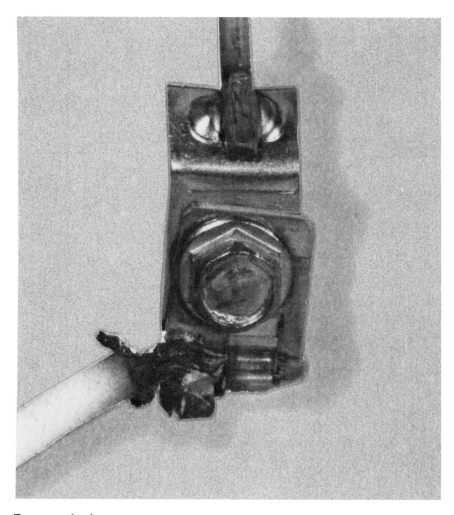

Damaged wire

Note: If replacement wire is required, use only appliance wire having the same temperature and gauge rating as the wire you are replacing. In most service replacements, this will be 16 gauge appliance wire with 150° C heat resistance except as noted in your range's circuit diagram.

5 continued

Step 1: Be sure all range controls are turned **OFF**. Disconnect the power supply at the distribution panel and unplug the range from the receptacle. Watch for sharp edges.

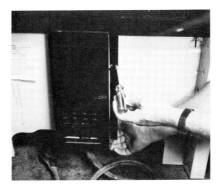

Step 2: This procedure requires the removal of access panels from your range. If you are unfamiliar with this process, please refer to Procedure #3: Removing Access and Control Panels.

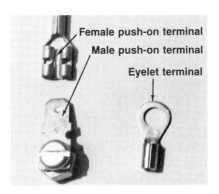

Step 3: High-temperature terminals are typical of those used in range applications. Shown above are male and female "push-on" terminals and eyelet terminal.

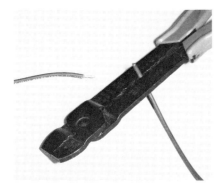

Step 4: To splice wiring, remove insulation from the wire. Preferably use wire strippers, since it is less likely to cut into the conductor than with a knife. Remove only enough insulation to allow you to make the connection or splice.

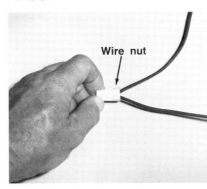

Step 5: Range wiring should be spliced only by using a ceramic high-temperature wire nut. Strip the insulation back to bright and shiny wire. Twist strands together, and secure with wire nut.

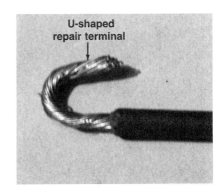

Step 6: U-shape repair terminal can be substituted for burned-off eyelet terminal, but never for push-on terminal.

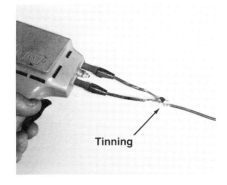

Step 7: To form U-shape terminal, strip wire about ½ inch and twist strands into a "U" shape. Use soldering gun and solder to "tin" (coat) standard wires.

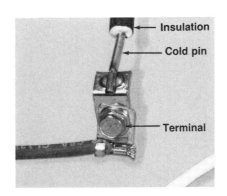

Step 8: When removing or replacing terminal screw, firmly hold the terminal in order not to bend cold pin. Cold pin should be centered in the insulation away from the sheath since bending could cause electrical short.

6 Inspecting and replacing single-coil plug-in surface units

Skill Level Rating:	Easy	**Average**	Difficult	Very Difficult

Because of its easy accessibility and simple electrical circuit, the single-coil plug-in type surface unit is easy to test and replace. An inner coil of nichrome wire, which does the actual heating, is completely surrounded by an insulating material. The inner coil is also covered with a metal sheath to greatly extend its life by reducing damage and oxidation. Since you can't see the internal coil which does the heating you have to rely on the ohmmeter to tell you when the unit is not working, except in those cases where damage is visible on the metal sheath or terminals.

Important Note: If your surface unit terminals are damaged or corroded, check the receptacle as described in Procedure 7: Inspecting and Replacing Surface Unit Receptacles. The receptacle contacts may also be damaged and should be replaced before installing a new surface unit.

Single-coil plug-in surface unit

6 continued

Step 1: Be sure all range controls are turned **OFF**. Disconnect the power supply at the distribution panel and unplug the range from the receptacle. Watch for sharp edges on cooktop surface and parts.

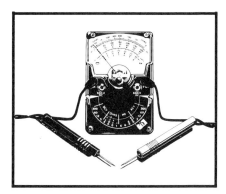

Step 2: This procedure requires the use of an ohmmeter. For instructions on how to use an ohmmeter, please refer to Tools and Testing Equipment, page 96.

Step 3: If surface unit fails to heat, remove plug-in unit by first lifting unit up about one inch from cooktop surface.

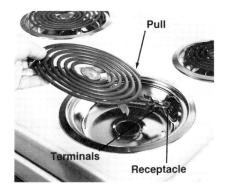

Step 4: With unit still in raised position, pull from receptacle. When removing from receptacle, avoid bending terminals.

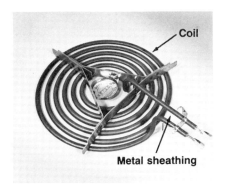

Step 5: When unit is removed, inspect thoroughly on top and underside. Look carefully at metal sheathing for signs of holes or burning that would indicate an internal malfunction. If this is found, unit must be replaced.

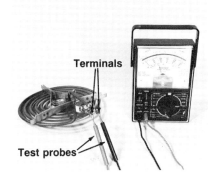

Step 6: To test for continuity, set ohmmeter to R x 1. Attach one test probe to each of the two terminals. Needle should read between 20 and 100 ohms. If no reading, replace unit.

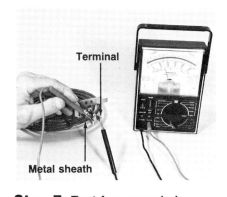

Step 7: Test for grounds by setting meter to R x 1 resistance setting. Attach one test probe to one unit terminal, while touching other test probe to metal sheath.

Step 8: If ohmmeter test indicates continuity, unit is grounded and should be replaced.

Step 9: To install new plug-in unit, insert terminals into receptacle. Be sure new unit fits evenly into cooktop surface.

7 Inspecting and replacing surface unit receptacles

Skill Level Rating:	Easy	**Average**	Difficult	Very Difficult

Plug-in surface units make electrical contact through the receptacle. Sometimes the problem with a non-heating surface unit is in the receptacle rather than the heating element. Receptacle faults are easy to diagnose since most are visible. The receptacle may need to be replaced as an entire unit or repaired with a spring contact parts kit.

If your receptacle contacts are damaged, check surface unit terminals as described in Procedure 6: Inspecting and Replacing Plug-in Surface Units. A corroded surface unit terminal will repeatedly damage receptacle contacts.

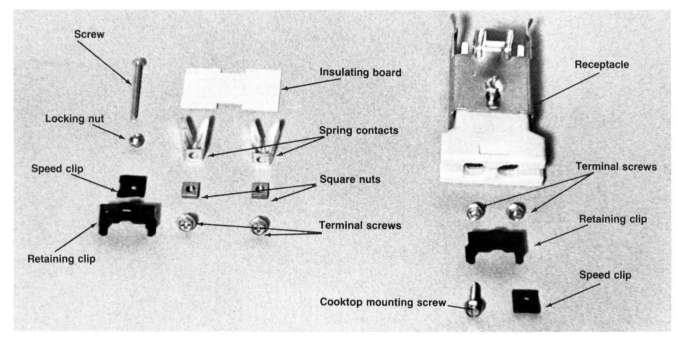

Receptacle replacement parts kits

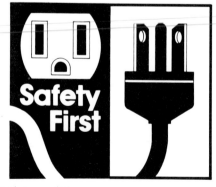

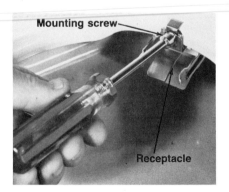

Step 1: Be sure all range controls are turned **OFF**. Disconnect the power supply at the distribution panel and unplug the range from the receptacle. Watch for sharp edges on cooktop surface and parts.

Step 2: Check to see if surface unit makes good contact with grounding flange. Adjust flange slightly with pliers to tighten contact.

Step 3: To inspect receptacle further, remove it from mounting tab by loosening single mounting screw. Pull through cooktop opening.

7 continued

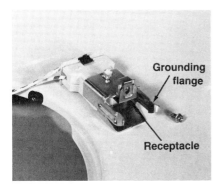

Step 4: Check lead wires to rear terminals for loose connection or corrosion. Tighten or replace as described in Procedure #5: Wiring and connections. If insulator block is cracked go to Step 6.

Step 5: Check condition of female spring contacts inside receptacle. If burnt, oxidized, or bent, replace contacts or entire receptacle.

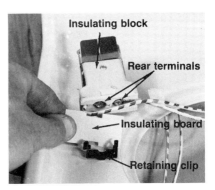

Step 6: To disconnect receptacle, remove retaining clip with screwdriver and lift out insulating board. Save board for receptacle replacement. Do not bend. If replacing entire receptacle go to Step 11.

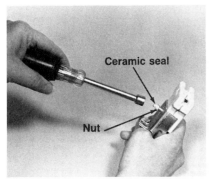

Step 7: If replacing contacts, use 5/16″ nutdriver to break ceramic seal on nut of screw holding receptacle together. CAUTION: Wear eye protection if you need pliers to break seal.

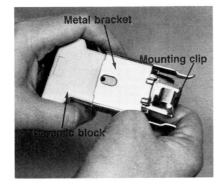

Step 8: Remove nut, spacer and screw. Slide ceramic block out of metal bracket and open. Remove old spring contacts and square nuts.

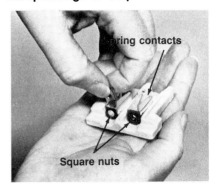

Step 9: Position new spring contacts with square nuts at wide end of ceramic clock. Put two halves of ceramic block back together.

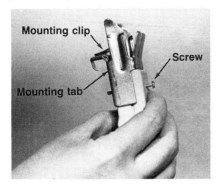

Step 10: Slide ceramic block into metal bracket with spring mounting clip over mounting tab between bracket and block. insert new screw up block and out through bracket. Put on spacer and tighten with special locking nut.

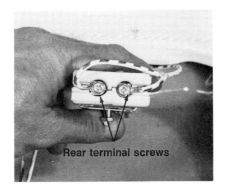

Step 11: Connect wires with new terminal screws. Cover terminals with insulating board and snap retainer in place.

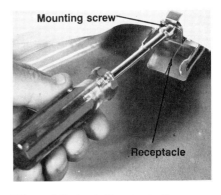

Step 12: Install speed clip over cooktop mounting hole with smaller opening behind hole and larger opening in front. Install receptacle, tightening mounting screw securely for proper grounding.

8 Inspecting and replacing one-coil wired type surface units

Skill Level Rating:	Easy	Average	**Difficult**	Very Difficult

The one-coil wired surface unit is used in conjunction with the infinite heat switch. Like the plug-in unit, it consists of only one unit that is "pulsed" by the switch to provide various levels of heat.

When inspecting a wired type surface unit, be sure that its two wiring terminals are tightly attached to the unit terminal. A special heat-resistant connector is used for this purpose.

Note: A one-coil wired type surface unit may be replaced with a two-coil wired type unit. Installation instructions come with the two-coil replacement unit.

One-coil wired type surface unit

Step 1: Be sure all range controls are turned **OFF**. Disconnect the power supply at the distribution panel and unplug the range from the receptacle. Watch for sharp edges on cooktop surface and parts.

Step 2: This procedure requires the use of an ohmmeter. For instructions on how to use an ohmmeter, please refer to Tools and Testing Equipment, page 96.

Step 3: If surface unit fails to heat, lift up unit and remove reflector pan. Inspect for damaged wiring at terminals, or an opening burned in unit. If damaged, replace unit.

Hinge clip

Step 4: To remove the unit, remove hinge clip screw at hinge and lift unit from range. Inspect insulating block around terminals for cracks or breaks. A damaged block can be dangerous and must be replaced.

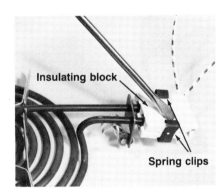

Insulating block

Spring clips

Step 5: Insulating block can be removed by snapping off two spring clips. Avoid damaging block when prying loose clips.

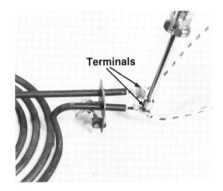

Terminals

Step 6: Remove one screw connected to either of the two unit terminals. Use care when loosening screw; avoid bending terminals. (For installation reference, make note of how wires are connected).

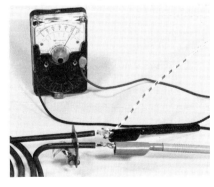

Step 7: To test for continuity, set ohmmeter to R x 1. With one lead removed, attach one test probe to disconnected terminal. Needle should read between 20 and 100 ohms.

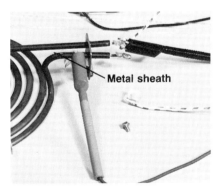

Metal sheath

Step 8: Test for grounds by setting ohmmeter to R x 1 resistance setting. Touch one test probe to unit terminal and other probe to metal sheath. No continuity should be measured.

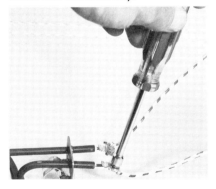

Step 9: Replace unit if either test for continuity or test for grounds indicates damage. To install new unit, attach wiring in same position as it was originally installed. Fasten hinge clip screw securely to insure proper grounding of unit.

9 Inspecting and replacing two-coil wired type heating units

Skill Level Rating:	Easy	Average	**Difficult**	Very Difficult

The two-coil wired type surface heating units are wired directly to the range rather than being connected to a plug-in receptacle. These units have a hinge arrangement so they can be lifted easily for cleaning. The wiring attaches to the three terminals of the unit with screws. Three wires lead to the two-coil unit. Two of the terminals are "bonded" together to form a common terminal, which is connected to the black lead wire. Wires from the switch attach to the other two terminals.

Two-coil wired type surface unit

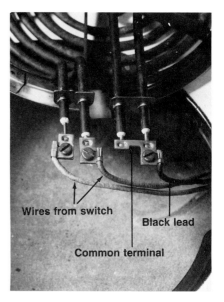

Close-up of connections

Step 1: Be sure all range controls are turned **OFF**. Disconnect the power supply at the distribution panel and unplug the range from the receptacle. Watch for sharp edges on cooktop surface and parts.

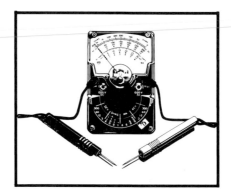

Step 2: This procedure requires the use of an ohmmeter. For instructions on how to use an ohmmeter, please refer to Tools and Testing Equipment, page 96.

Step 3: If surface unit fails to heat, lift up the unit and remove reflector pan. Inspect for damaged wiring at terminals, or an opening burned in unit. If damaged, replace unit.

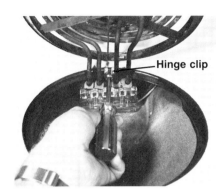

Step 4: To remove the unit, loosen the screw at the hinge clip. When the screw is loosened, the hinge drops down to free the unit.

Step 5: Some terminals are covered with a glass or ceramic insulating block that must be removed to expose the connections. Check block for cracks or breaks. A damaged block can be dangerous and must be replaced.

Step 6: To remove the insulating block, remove the two spring clips from each end of the block. The two halves will separate to expose the wiring connections.

Step 7: Unscrew wires from terminals. Use care when loosening screw; avoid bending terminals. (For installation reference, make note of how wires are connected).

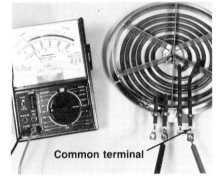

Step 8: To test for continuity set ohmmeter to R x 1. Touch test probes between common terminal and one of the other two terminals. Needle should read between 20 and 100 ohms. If no reading, replace unit.

Step 9: Leave one probe attached to the common terminal and move second probe to terminal of other coil. Again, needle should move partially upscale to indicate resistance of coil.

Step 10: Check for grounds with meter on R x 1 resistance setting. Touch one test probe to one of the three terminals and other probe to metal sheath of unit. No continuity should be measured.

Step 11: Repeat test for grounds for remaining two terminals. If needle moves upscale, ground fault is present and unit should be replaced.

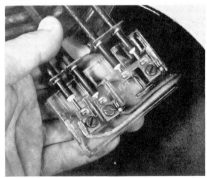

Step 12: To install new unit, attach wiring in same position as it was originally installed. Be sure insulator blocks and hinge clip are reinstalled properly. Fasten hinge clip screw securely to insure proper grounding of unit.

10 Inspecting and replacing three-coil wired type surface units

Skill Level Rating:	Easy	Average	**Difficult**	Very Difficult

The three-coil wired type surface unit allows you to adjust the number of coils energized to the size of the cooking utensil. This results in increased cooking efficiency. A coil size selector switch is used to regulate the three-coil circuit. The inner (small coil) circuitry does not pass through this switch since it is always energized when the surface unit control switch is turned to the "ON" position. Turning the coil size selector to the 6-inch position energizes the middle coil, and by turning the selector switch to the 8-inch position all three coils are energized. The heat level of all three coils is controlled by the surface unit switch.

Three-coil wired type surface unit

10 continued

Step 1: Be sure all range controls are turned **OFF**. Disconnect the power supply at the distribution panel and unplug the range from the receptacle. Watch for sharp edges on cooktop surface and parts.

Step 2: This procedure requires the use of an ohmmeter. For instructions on how to use an ohmmeter, please refer to Tools and Testing Equipment, page 96.

Step 3: If surface unit fails to heat, lift up unit and remove reflector pan. Inspect wires and unit for damage. Check insulating block for cracks or breaks. A damaged block can be dangerous and must be replaced.

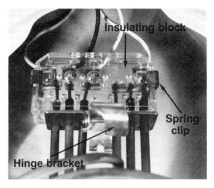

Step 4: To remove three-coil surface unit, loosen hinge bracket screw and push bracket down. Remove insulated glass block by removing two spring clips from each end; separate block into halves to expose the wiring connections.

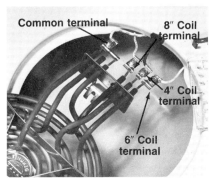

Step 5: Four wires connect to terminals; one wire to common terminal, three wires to corresponding terminals. Use care when loosening screw; avoid bending terminals. (For installation reference, make note of how wires are connected).

Step 6: To test for continuity, set ohmmeter to R x 1. Attach one test probe to common terminal; touch second probe to each of other three terminals. Needle should read between 20 and 100 ohms for each of the three test points.

Step 7: Test for grounds by setting ohmmeter to R x 1 resistance setting. Touch one test probe to metal sheath of unit. Touch other probe to each of the four terminals in turn. No continuity should be measured.

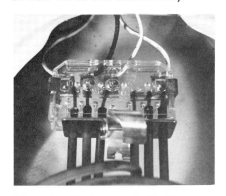

Step 8: Replace unit if either test indicates damage. To install new unit, attach wiring in same position as it was originally installed. Fasten hinge clip screw securely to insure proper grounding of unit.

11 Inspecting and replacing fixed-heat surface unit switch

Skill Level Rating:	Easy	Average	Difficult	**Very Difficult**

Many ranges use fixed-heat surface unit switches with either pushbutton or rotary-type controls. Used in conjunction with a 2-coil surface unit, the fixed-heat switch gives the range five different heat levels by switching between voltage selections and coil circuitry. The rotary fixed-heat switch is found behind the surface unit control knob of the backsplash or control panel. The inspection and replacement procedure is similar for both pushbutton and rotary fixed-heat switches.

Often an inoperative pushbutton surface unit will give outward indications that it has failed. Look for loose or overheated terminals. Also, mechanical malfunctions can prevent the pushbutton from operating correctly. Only one button should be depressed at a time; depressing any other button should cancel and raise the one which was originally in the down position. A switch which is jammed or mechanically inoperative should be replaced.

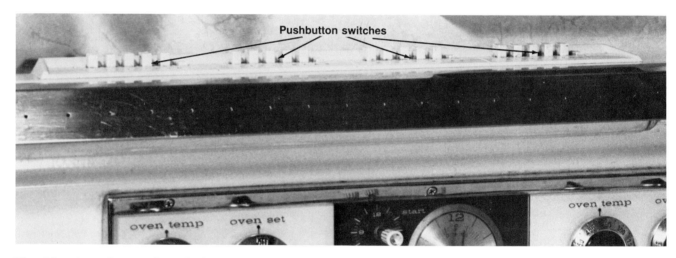

Fixed-heat surface unit switches

Step 1: Be sure all range controls are turned **OFF**. Disconnect the power supply at the distribution panel and unplug the range from the receptacle. Watch for sharp edges on cooktop surface and parts.

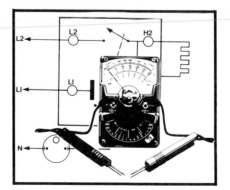

Step 2: This procedure requires the use of an ohmmeter and the ability to read a circuit diagram. For instructions, please refer to Tools and Testing Equipment, pages 96-98.

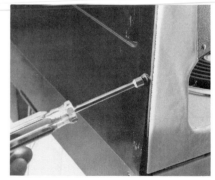

Step 3: This procedure requires the removal of access panels from your range. If you are unfamiliar with this process, please refer to Procedure #3: Removing Access and Control Panels.

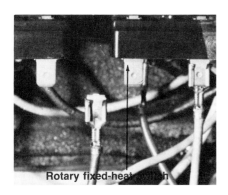

Rotary fixed-heat switch

Step 4: With rear access panel removed, switch can be tested while in range. Remove all push-on leads before testing. (For installation reference, make note of how wires are connected).

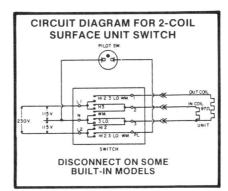

CIRCUIT DIAGRAM FOR 2-COIL SURFACE UNIT SWITCH

PILOT SW.

OUT COIL
IN COIL 97Ω
UNIT

230 V.
115 V
115 V

SWITCH

DISCONNECT ON SOME BUILT-IN MODELS

Step 5: Pushbutton and rotary switches have same internal circuitry except on Sensi-Temp™ units. Markings indicate setting in which switch contacts should be closed, indicating continuity when checked with ohmmeter.

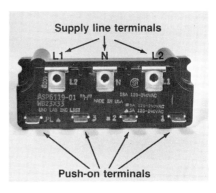

Supply line terminals

L1   N   L2

Push-on terminals

Step 6: Use ohmmeter to test from supply line terminals to push-on unit terminals for continuity at each position. Supply line terminals are marked L1, L2 and N.

Test probes

Step 7: Meter should sweep completely to 0, indicating continuity, when contacts are closed. If test shows failure, replace switch.

Trim panel

oven temp   oven set

Step 8: To replace pushbutton switch, remove trim panel that surrounds switch. Remove clip fasteners and carefully pry up trim with hand. (Do not use knife or screwdriver; trim may bend or break).

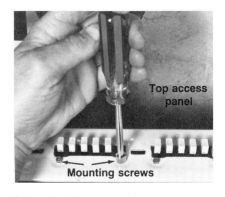

Top access panel

Mounting screws

Step 9: Unscrew mounting screws and remove remaining wires from switch. (For installation reference, make note of how wires are connected).

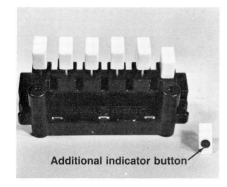

Additional indicator button

Step 10: Replacement switches usually have an additional pushbutton with red indicator dot. Use indicator button as "OFF" button for ranges without pilot lights.

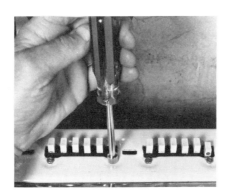

Step 11: To install new pushbutton switch, connect terminal wires to switch terminals. Replace top access panels, mounting screws and trim panel.

12 Inspecting and replacing infinite-heat surface unit switch

Skill Level Rating:	Easy	**Average**	Difficult	Very Difficult

Ranges with single-coil surface units use a rotary infinite-heat switch. This switch is characterized by the lack of "stops" between HI and WARM positions. Such stops are unnecessary because an infinite number of heat ranges are available between those two levels.

This switch is designed to "pulse" electrical current to the surface unit. The ratio of "on" to "off" time determines the heat output. One of the contact arms inside the switch is made from two strips of metal bonded together and is called a bimetal arm. A small heater surrounds the bimetal arm. When the switch is turned on, heat acting upon the bimetal arm produces a bending or warping effect that eventually opens the contacts, causing the current to stop flowing to both the surface unit and the internal heater. When the arm cools slightly, it again makes contact.

Turning the knob moves a cam that adjusts the tension on the bimetal arm and thus determines the amount of heat required to open the contacts. At the HI setting the contacts are constantly closed. As the knob is turned to the lower settings, the relationship of "on" time becomes less and "off" time becomes greater.

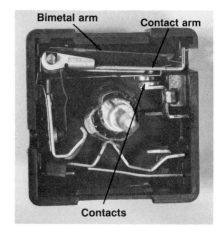

Infinite-heat surface unit switch

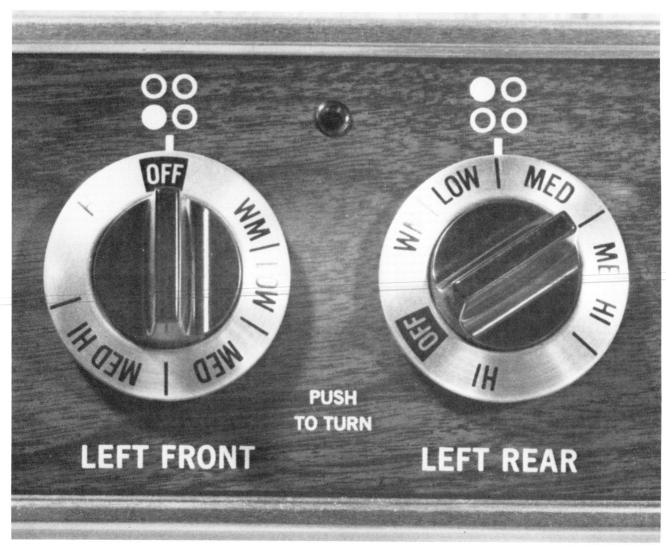

Infinite-heat switch control knob

Step 1: Be sure all range controls are turned **OFF**. Disconnect the power supply at the distribution panel and unplug the range from the receptacle. Watch for sharp edges.

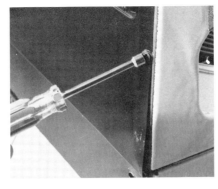

Step 2: This procedure requires the removal of access panels from your range. If you are unfamiliar with this process, please refer to Procedure #3: Removing Access and Control Panels.

Step 3: If unit is on high at all switch settings, switch should be replaced. This is due to internal failure of switch and cannot be repaired.

Step 4: If surface unit produces no heat but checks good, remove rear access panel. Examine terminal wires to switch. If terminals appear all right, switch should be replaced.

Step 5: Remove knob by pulling it straight off the switch shaft. On some models a spring clip on the back of the knob retains knob in place.

Step 6: After knob is removed, two screws can be seen adjacent to knob shaft. Remove these two screws.

Step 7: From rear of control panel, pull switch free from mounting position.

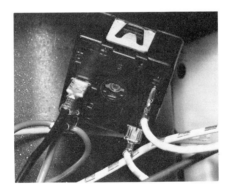

Step 8: Disconnect wires from switch. (For installation reference, make note of how wires are connected).

Step9: To install new switch, reverse Steps 6-9. Be sure "TOP" reference marked on switch is in upright position.

13 Inspecting and replacing surface unit coil size selector switch

Skill Level Rating:	Easy	**Average**	Difficult	Very Difficult

The size selector switch allows you to save energy by heating only the contact area directly beneath a cooking utensil. It is used with the three-coil surface unit, allowing selection of a 4-inch, 6-inch, or 8-inch diameter heating area.

The inner 4-inch coil is not controlled by the size selector switch. The smallest coil is always energized when the surface unit control is "ON". Turning the size selector switch to the 6-inch position energizes the middle coil as well. The 8-inch position energizes the outer coil in addition to the other two coils.

Note: If the 6-inch middle and/or 8-inch outer surface unit coils fail to heat, size selector switch may be defective.

Size selector switch

13 continued

Step 1: Be sure all range controls are turned **OFF**. Disconnect the power supply at the distribution panel and unplug the range from the receptacle. Watch for sharp edges.

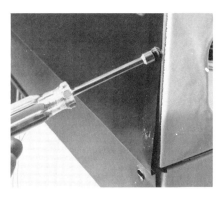

Step 2: This procedure requires the removal of access panels from your range. If you are unfamiliar with this process, please refer to Procedure #3: Removing Access and Control Panels.

Step 3: With top rear access panel removed, size selector switch can be inspected in range. Inspect terminals visually for oxidation or discoloring. If wiring terminals are damaged, replace terminals.

Step 4: If surface unit tests good and visual inspection of switch wiring is all right, but surface unit fails to operate in 6″ and/or 8″ position, replace size selector switch.

Step 5: To replace switch, remove size selector switch control knob from control panel. Remove switch mounting screws. (On some ranges it will be necessary to remove front glass panel for access to screws.)

Step 6: Remove switch from rear and disconnect wiring. (For installation reference, make note of how wires are connected.) Install new switch, connecting wires as in original position. Fasten new switch in place with mounting screws.

14 Inspecting and replacing automatic Sensi-Temp™ surface unit

Skill Level Rating:	Easy	Average	**Difficult**	Very Difficult

The automatic Sensi-Temp™ surface unit uses a variety of complex components to allow precise control of cooking temperature. The control knob sets the control, called a responder, for the desired temperature. The responder turns power to the surface unit on and off in a cycling action that keeps a utensil at the selected temperature.

A sensor in the center of the surface unit reaches the same temperature as a utensil placed on the unit. Inside the sensor, a resistor-type sensing element changes value in proportion to its temperature. This change in value alters the current flow from sensor to responder. A 12-volt transformer provides the power for this control circuit. The control circuit activates the responder to cycle the surface unit on and off.

Proper contact between the bottom of the utensil and the sensor is important. Only flat-bottomed utensils should be used on the Sensi-Temp™ unit. Use utensils that correspond in size to the size of the unit. If your range has a size selector switch for the Sensi-Temp™ unit, use it to heat only the area needed.

Sensi-Temp™ surface unit

Step 1: Be sure all range controls are turned **OFF**. Disconnect the power supply at the distribution panel and unplug the range from receptacle. Watch for sharp edges.

Step 2: This procedure requires the use of an ohmmeter. For instructions on how to use an ohmmeter, please refer to Tools and Testing Equipment, page 96.

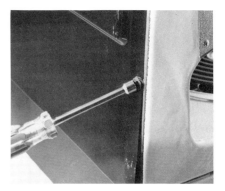

Step 3: This procedure requires removal of access panels from range. If you are unfamiliar with the process, please refer to Procedure #3: Removing Access and Control Panels.

Step 4: Lift surface unit and visually inspect sensor for physical damage or broken connections. Sensor should move easily when depressed by hand.

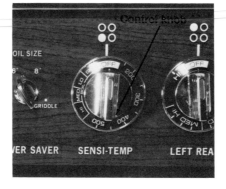

Step 5: To test sensor, locate leads connecting it to the responder. Remove access panel. Responder is located directly behind Sensi-Temp™ control knob on control panel or backsplash.

Step 6: Locate terminals S and TS on responder. Set ohmmeter to R x 1. Remove lead from terminal S. Attach one probe to S and other to TS terminal. Meter should move upscale to approximately 15 ohms.

14 continued

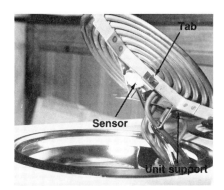

Step7: If meter needle does not move, replace sensor. Remove sensor from surface unit by removing screws on tabs which fasten it to unit support.

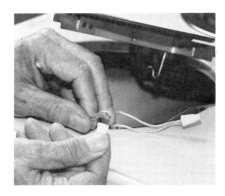

Step 8: Cut leads near sensor. Strip insulation from remaining leads about ½ inch. Install sensor using special connectors supplied with part. Push excess wire beneath cooktop, out of drain basin.

Step 9: If sensor is good, set ohmmeter to R x 1 and test transformer. Two leads run from transformer to responder. Remove one lead from transformer and test between these two terminals.

Step 10: Repeat test on remaining two transformer terminals. Needle should sweep partially upscale for both tests. If either test fails, replace transformer. (For installation reference, make note of how wires are connected.)

Step 11: Sensi-Temp™ surface unit is tested as if it were an ordinary three-coil wired type unit. Follow instructions outlined in Procedure #10: Inspecting and Replacing Three-Coil Wired Type Surface Units.

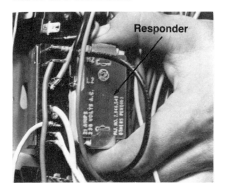

Step 12: The responder, the only other component involved in the Sensi-Temp™ operation, cannot be easily tested. If sensor, transformer, and surface unit all test good, replace responder.

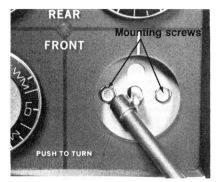

Step 13: To replace responder, pull off Sensi-Temp™ unit control knob. Remove mounting screws beneath knob and locate responder inside control panel. Label wire leads for installation reference then remove. Lift out responder.

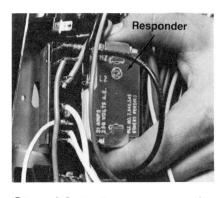

Step 14: Fasten new responder into place. Transfer wiring to new responder, one lead at a time, making same connections as on original responder.

15 Inspecting oven vent

Skill Level Rating: | **Easy** | Average | Difficult | Very Difficult |

The oven vent is located in the top of the oven. A baffle may be at the lower end of the vent opening to limit air movement out of the oven cavity. After the heated air leaves the vent tube, the vent passageway directs the air to an area beneath one of the surface units.

Note: On all self-cleaning ranges, a metal grid called a smoke eliminator is positioned at the bottom of the oven vent. Do not attempt to remove this component.

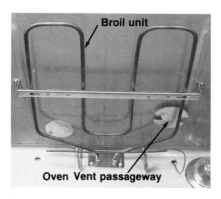

Oven vent

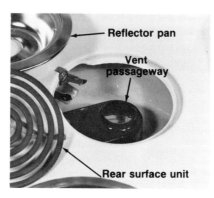

Step 1: Be sure all range controls are turned **OFF**. Disconnect the power supply at the distribution panel and unplug the range from the receptacle. Watch for sharp edges on oven vent.

Step 2: Remove rear surface unit. Look for oven vent passageway located beneath it. Passageway can be lifted out and pulled free.

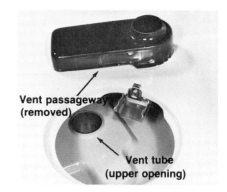

Step 3: With vent passageway removed, top of vent tube is visible. Most blockages from foreign objects will occur near the top of the tube opening.

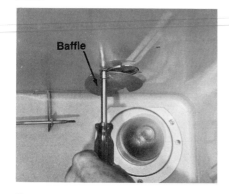

Step 4: Lower end of tube can be checked after lower baffle is removed from inside the oven cavity. Loosen screws on either side of baffle plate to release lower baffle.

Step 5: Be sure oven vent passageway is replaced properly. Round hole in vent passageway must be in line with round hole in reflector pan. If dislocated, heat could travel improperly throughout top of range.

16 Adjusting oven door

Skill Level Rating: | **Easy** | Average | Difficult | Very Difficult |

It is important for air currents in the oven to follow certain paths to obtain consistent temperatures. If this pattern is disrupted, oven temperatures can vary and foods cooked in different locations in the oven may not be consistent.

The oven door is semi-flexible. It can be adjusted to compensate for various conditions of range cabinet position and movement. However, if the range cabinet is not level, the door may be warped and will not seal properly. A misaligned oven door can result in heat escaping from oven, causing signs of smoke leakage around door frame.

Step 1: Be sure all controls are turned **OFF**. Disconnect the power supply at the distribution panel and unplug the range from the receptacle. Watch for sharp edges.

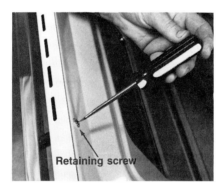

Retaining screw

Step 2: Slightly loosen all screws that retain the inner and outer door panels together. This would include loosening the two screws that hold the door handle.

Step 3: By grasping the door at the top, exert a slight twisting force left to right to adjust door properly. Retighten screws. Be careful not to overtighten, causing the porcelain to chip. Make adjustments several times if necessary until door aligns properly with range cabinet.

Step 4: When door fits correctly, a light push against both top corners should result only in slight movement of door. If door is not properly adjusted, repeat Step 3.

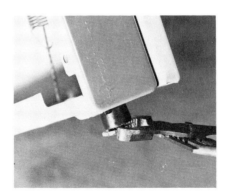

Step 5: To level range, locate leveling screws at each corner of range front. Remove bottom drawer and use pliers to turn screw to proper adjustment.

17 Inspecting and replacing oven door glass

Skill Level Ruling: | Easy | Average | **Difficult** | Very Difficult

The oven door glass is a popular feature because it allows you to view the food without opening the oven door. The glass is "double glazed" to reduce heat loss through the glass in normal use. Tempered glass is used to prevent breakage under the extreme heat encountered in an oven.

In many models, one glass is fastened to the inner door panel and a second to the outer panel with a frame between the two. Others have a glass "plug" assembly sandwiched between the inner and outer door panels. Some ranges have a full-width glass which forms the outer door panel. In self-cleaning ovens, a special door shield is used that must be in place during cleaning operations.

To clean the inner glass surface or to replace a broken glass panel, it is necessary to disassemble the oven door. Use care when handling both the porcelain-coated panels and the glass to prevent damage. When replacing glass do not overtighten screws; this may stress the glass and cause it to break when heated. Also, never replace broken glass with ordinary window glass.

Step 1: Be sure all range controls are turned **OFF**. Disconnect the power supply at the distribution panel and unplug the range from the receptacle. Watch for sharp edges on oven door glass.

Step 2: For easy access, remove oven door. Some models have lift-off doors; others require removal of support screws. Use caution when working around hinge post. Post is under spring tension and may snap shut.

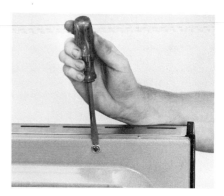

Step 3: Remove screws from inner door panel that hold inner and outer panels of door together. These screws may also hold door handle in place.

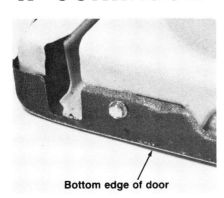

Bottom edge of door

Step 4: Examine bottom edge of door for other screws that may hold panels together. Do not force panels apart since this may damage porcelain.

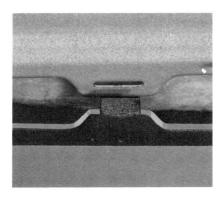

Step 5: With all door panel retaining screws removed, panels may be separated. Outer panel has tabs at bottom which insert into slots of inner panel. Start at top of door panel and lift door panel free from tabs.

Step 6: With panels separated, you can reach the inner surface of glass assembly. Note position of insulation and use caution to insure proper replacement.

INSIDE

Step 7: Glass assembly consists of different kinds of temperature sensitive glass. Each pane of glass should be identified before disassembly to be certain the same piece is reassembled in the same location.

Step 8: Disassemble glass panel from door by removing support brackets. Some doors may have sealed glass frame package and if broken must be replaced as a complete package.

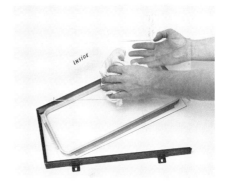

Step 9: To clean glass panels, use liquid dishwashing detergent and warm water. If food soils are baked on, non-abrasive oven cleaner can be used.

Rope gasket

Step 10: To clean sealed glass frame package, carefully loosen wrap around frame. Identify each panel of glass for reassembly. Clean glass as instructed in Step 9. When reinstalling glass panels into frame, be sure rope gasket is in proper place.

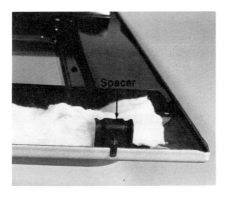

Spacer

Step 11: Spacers are used on some doors to provide proper distance between inner and outer panels. Be sure they are clipped to door edge and in place.

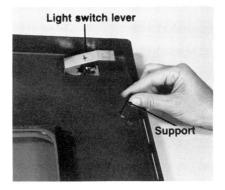

Light switch lever

Support

Step 12: Spacer may be used on screw bolts that hold handle in place. Hold screw in position, then drop spacer over screw before reassembling inner and outer panels.

18 Inspecting and replacing oven gaskets

Skill Level Rating:	Easy	Average	**Difficult**	Very Difficult

The oven gasket plays a major part in controlling the proper air flow in the oven. It is not intended to seal the oven nor to make it air tight. In most cases, it surrounds only the upper portion of the oven cavity, allowing air to enter from the bottom.

The oven gasket is made of special high-temperature material and may be attached to either the door or the body of the oven. If the gasket is torn or missing, it should be replaced so that air cannot escape and affect the cooking performance of the oven.

There are two types of oven gaskets. Gaskets can be mounted either to the oven body or to the oven door. Only self-cleaning ranges have gaskets mounted to the oven door.

Note: On some models, oven gaskets are not present.

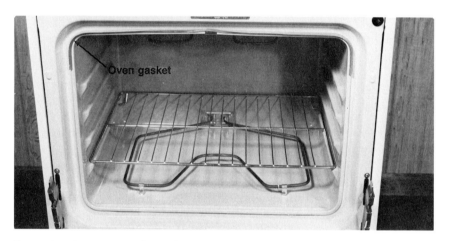

Oven body-mounted gasket

Oven door-mounted gasket

Step 1: Be sure all range controls are turned **OFF**. Disconnect the power supply at the distribution panel and unplug the range from the receptacle. Watch for sharp edges.

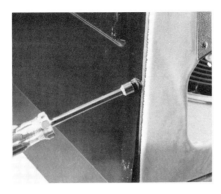

Step 2: This procedure may require the removal of rear access panels from your range. If you are unfamiliar with this process, please refer to Procedure #3: Removing Access and Control Panels.

Step 3: Body Mounted. For easy access, remove oven door. Some models have lift-off door; others require removal of support screws. Use caution when working around a hinge post. Post is under spring tension and may snap shut.

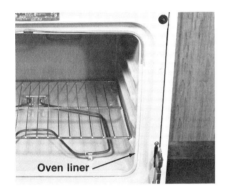

Step 4: To remove damaged oven gasket from oven body, range oven liner must be loosened. There are three general types of oven liner mountings: (1) front side screws; (2) rear "J" bolts; and (3) rear spring.

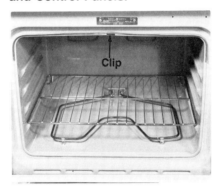

Step 5: To loosen oven liner fastened to front frame by side screws, remove two screws located at front of oven on the two sides. On some models you may have to remove a clip at top front of oven liner.

Step 6: If your range has no side screws at front of oven liner, liner is held by "J" bolt or rear spring type mountings. Only loosening "J" bolt mounting will be explained, since spring type mounting requires special tools and qualified service technician.

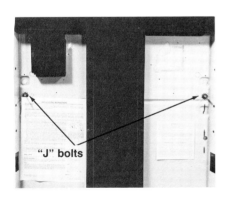

Step 7: On some ranges, you may have to remove back access panels to locate J-bolts that retain oven cavity in place. J-bolts are large bolts that protrude from the middle sides of the range body.

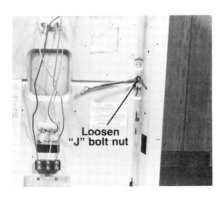

Step 8: Loosen nuts on J-bolts about ¼ of an inch. Hold end of bolt and use wrench to loosen nut until oven liner can be pulled forward about ⅛ of an inch away from range body.

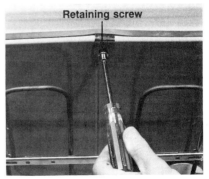

Step 9: Returning to front of cabinet, examine front edge of oven liner for any retaining screws or gasket clips.

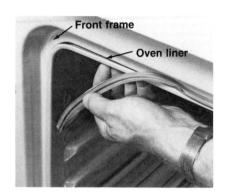

Step 10: Grasping inner surface of oven liner, rock liner back and forth until it moves forward about ⅛-inch, releasing gasket from clamped position between liner and front frame. Gasket can now be pulled free.

Step 11: Install new gasket in position between oven liner and range body. Be sure lip of gasket is behind flange of oven liner before pushing liner back into position and tightening J-bolts.

Step 12: Door Mounted. On self-cleaning ovens, braided gasket is attached to oven door. If gasket is broken or damaged, it should be replaced. For easier access to gasket, remove oven door.

Step 13: On self-cleaning ranges there are several types of gaskets mounted to oven door. Replacement procedures will be similar for all gaskets.

Step 14: Door panels must be separated before gasket can be removed. Remove screws from inner door panel that hold inner and outer panels of door together (these screws may also hold door handle in place).

Step 15: Examine edges of door for other screws that hold panels together. Do not force panels apart since this may damage porcelain.

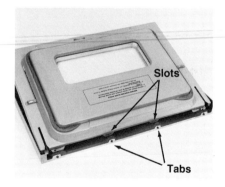

Step 16: With all door panel retaining screws removed, panels can now be separated. Outer door panel has tabs which insert into slots at the bottom of inner door panel. Start at top of door panel and lift door panel free from tabs.

Step 17: To replace damaged braided gasket on models having window door, remove the complete window shield assembly. This allows access to retainer panel which holds gasket to door.

Step 18: Remove all retainer screws from retainer panel. Carefully slip gasket out of retainer. Note position of insulation and use caution to assure proper replacement.

18 continued

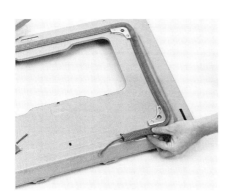

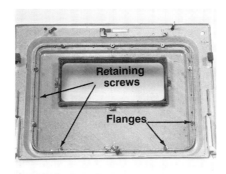

Step 19: To install new gasket, dress gasket under retainer and reset retaining screws. Be sure to properly reassemble window shield assembly and door panels.

Step 20: On some doors, gasket is held between flanges of two separate panels. To remove gasket from this type door, remove retaining screws and separate two panels.

Step 21: To install new gasket, position gasket with small gasket bead seated on edge of flange. Press panels together and reset two center side retaining screws. Adjust gasket if necessary for appearance and install remaining screws.

19 Inspecting and replacing oven door hinges

Skill Level Rating:

Easy	Average	**Difficult**	Very Difficult

The oven door hinge plays a major part in the operation of the oven. It adjusts the height of the door and controls the stopping point in the broil and open position. It also determines the "feel" of the oven door. A hinge in good condition makes for smooth, secure oven door operation. One that is worn can make the door movement weak and wobbly.

Oven door disassembly is not required to replace a worn or broken hinge. With the lift-off door feature, the hinge remains mounted to the oven cabinet and slides into a socket in the oven door.

Note: There are four general types of oven door hinge assemblies. Since there are similarities in adjusting these four door hinges, Procedure 19 will use only one type of hinge assembly as an example.

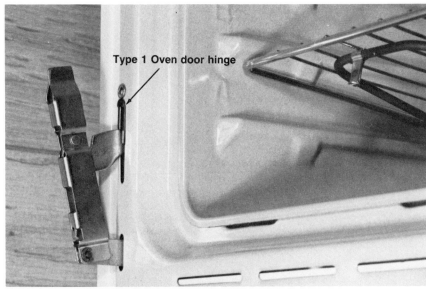

Type 1 Oven door hinge

Oven door hinges

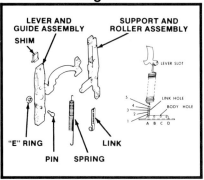

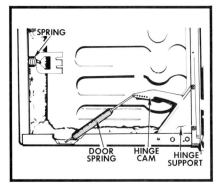

Type 1: Found on most free-standing 30″ and hi/low models. Door balance and tension can both be adjusted by moving spring.

Type 2: Found on some 30″ free-standing and built-in models. Door is adjusted by moving spring into one of the various holes in hinge assembly.

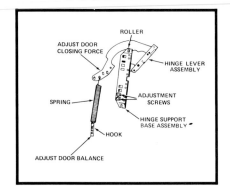

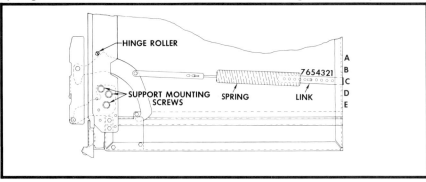

Type 3: Found mounted to body of most 40″ models. Door closing force is adjusted by moving spring into one of the hinge lever assembly holes. Balance can be adjusted by moving spring into one of the holes in hook.

Type 4: Found on most built-in wall ovens. Door is adjusted by positioning spring into various holes in the link.

19 continued

Step 1: Be sure all range controls are turned **OFF**. Disconnect the power supply at the distribution panel and unplug the range from the receptacle. Watch for sharp edges.

Step 2: On some built-in models in order to access the hinge assembly, it is necessary to partially move the range forward from the cabinet.

Step 3: To reach door hinges on ovens, remove four mounting screws (on some models, screws are under oven gasket). Using two people, slide oven partially out of its wooden cabinet. Be sure oven is balanced properly before opening oven door.

Step 4: To access some built-in ranges, remove four thumb screws located under each of the four surface units. Next, remove two end cap screws which hold metal trim shield in place. Slide trim shield down and pull range partially out.

Step 5: For easy access to hinge assembly, remove oven door. Some models have lift-off doors; other models require removal of support screws. Use caution when working around hinge post. Post is under tension and may snap shut.

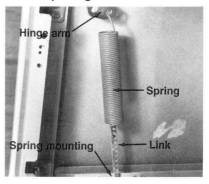

Step 6: Inspect hinge assembly. If assembly is broken, remove the range storage drawer. Note carefully the position of spring mounting for reinstallation.

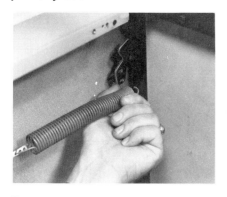

Step 7: Grasp spring and remove from hinge arm. Use care not to let spring slip.

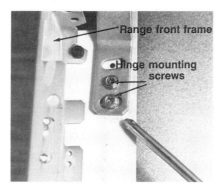

Step 8: On some models hinge mounting screws can be removed from storage drawer access area. For installation reference, note position of screws.

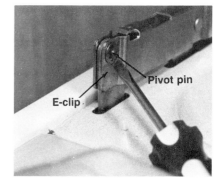

Step 9: Use screwdriver to remove E-clip from pivot pin located on front frame of range. Wear protective goggles and be careful of E-clip flying loose.

19 continued

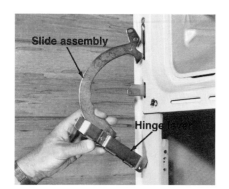

Step 10: After pivot pin is removed, hinge lever and slide assembly can be lifted out of range body in front.

Step 11: With hinge lever out of the way, loosen screw that retains roller and support on front frame of range body.

Step 12: With support screw removed, remainder of hinge assembly can be removed through storage access drawer opening.

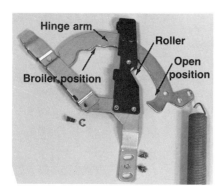

Step 13: Complete hinge assembly shows details of Type 1 assembly. Spring-loaded hinge arm moves against roller to retain door in either broil or open position.

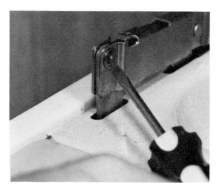

Step 14: When installing new hinge assembly, be sure to place spring in original position. To check for correct door alignment, refer to Procedure #16: Oven Door Adjustment.

Notes

20 Inspecting and replacing oven bake unit

| Skill Level Rating: | Easy | Average | Difficult | Very Difficult |

The bake unit is located at the bottom of the oven cavity. When the unit is energized, it heats the air in the oven and causes convection currents to be set up. Air circulation from the air intake around the door, through the oven interior, and out the top vent provides consistent cooking temperatures.

Bake unit

Oven bake unit

20 continued

Step 1: Be sure all range controls are turned **OFF**. Disconnect the power supply at the distribution panel and unplug the range from the receptacle. Watch for sharp edges on bake unit.

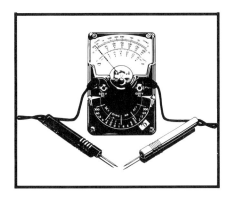

Step 2: This procedure requires the use of an ohmmeter. For instructions on how to use an ohmmeter, please refer to Tools and Testing Equipment, page 96.

Step 3: For easy access, remove oven door. Some models have lift-off doors; others require removal of support screws. Use caution when working around hinge post. Post is under spring tension and may snap shut.

Step 4: Lift up bake unit from bottom of oven as you would for cleaning. Remove two screws that fasten rear support to the back of oven cavity.

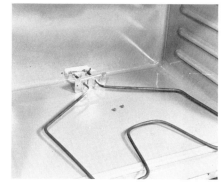

Step 5: With support bracket screws removed, gently pull bake unit forward several inches. Inspect wiring connections carefully. Check for signs of burned wiring; terminals should be shiny and bright.

Step 6: Remove wiring terminals from unit. Use care when loosening screws, avoid bending terminals. (For installation reference, make note of how wires are connected).

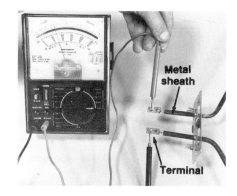

Step 7: With bake unit removed, test for continuity by setting ohmmeter to R x 1 position. Place test probes at each terminal. Needle should read between 15 and 30 ohms. If no reading, replace unit.

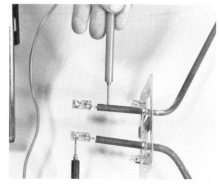

Step 8: Test for grounds by setting meter to R x 1 resistance setting. Place one test probe on one terminal and other probe to metal sheath of unit. If needle moves upscale, unit is grounded and should be replaced.

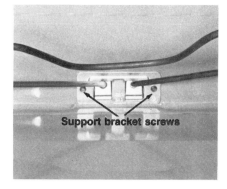

Step 9: To install new unit, attach wiring in same position as it was originally installed. Fasten support bracket screws securely to insure proper grounding of unit.

21 Inspecting and replacing oven broil unit

Skill Level Rating:	Easy	Average	**Difficult**	Very Difficult

The broil unit is located at the top of the oven cavity. It serves as a radiant heater to cook foods placed immediately below it.

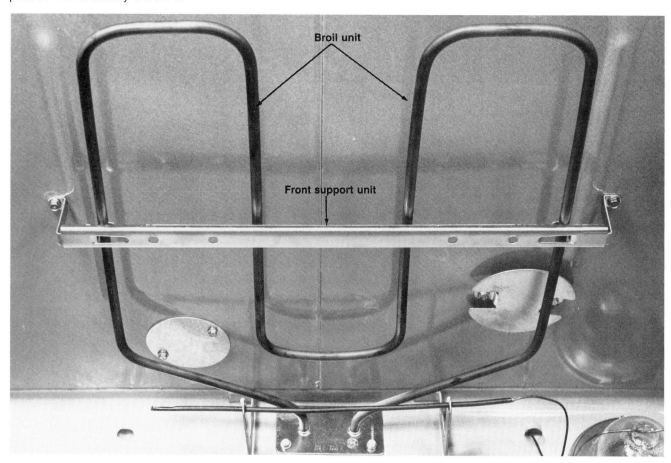

Oven broil unit

Step 1: Be sure all range controls are turned **OFF**. Disconnect the power supply at the distribution panel and unplug the range from the receptacle. Watch for sharp edges on broil unit.

Step 2: This procedure requires the use of an ohmmeter. For instructions on how to use an ohmmeter, please refer to Tools and Testing, page 96.

Step 3: For easy access, remove oven door. Some models have lift-off doors; others require removal of support screws. Use caution when working around hinge post. Post is under spring tension and may snap shut.

21 continued

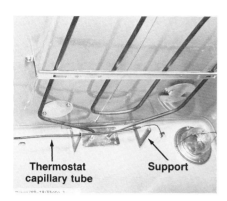

Thermostat capillary tube   Support

Step 4: If capillary tube is in the way, it must be moved. Caution: In self-cleaning ovens, a caustic substance is used in the tube. Tube should be handled very carefully and only while using rubber gloves.

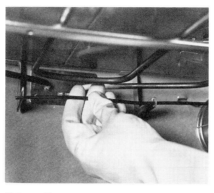

Step 5: To move tube lift smaller part of tube through slot in support or unclip tube from support. With rear of tube clear, front can slide back to free it from support. Do not bend or kink tube.

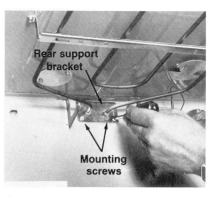

Rear support bracket

Mounting screws

Step 6: Rear support bracket mounting screws are now clear of obstruction and can be removed with nutdriver.

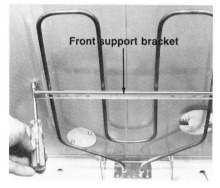

Front support bracket

Step 7: Front support bracket can be loosened by removing screws on either side. Broil unit can then be pulled forward several inches from rear wall.

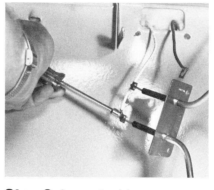

Step 8: Inspect wiring connections carefully for burned or damaged wires. Remove wiring terminals from unit. Use care when loosening screws, avoid bending terminals. (For installation reference, make note of how wires are connected).

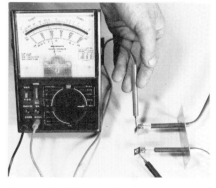

Step 9: With broil unit removed, test for continuity by setting ohmmeter to R x 1 position. Place test probes at each terminal. Needle should read between 15 and 30 ohms. If no reading, replace unit.

Step 10: Test for grounds by setting meter to R x 1 resistance setting. Place one probe on one terminal and other probe to metal sheath of broil unit. If needle moves upscale, replace unit.

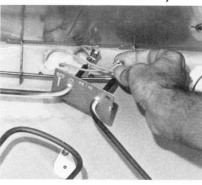

Step 11: To install new unit, attach wiring in same position as it was originally installed. Fasten support bracket screws securely to insure proper grounding of unit. Be sure thermostat tube is properly repositioned.

22 Inspecting and replacing oven selector switches

Skill Level Rating:	Easy	Average	Difficult	**Very Difficult**

The oven selector switch controls the function of the oven, causing either the bake or broil unit to be energized as required. It can also select "timed baked" on models equipped with automatic timers, allowing the timer to start and end the baking cycle at preset times.

The oven selector switch for self-cleaning ovens differs from that on conventional ovens by the addition of several contacts to energize the cleaning function. All of these functions are performed in conjunction with the thermostat, which controls the temperature level of the oven.

Because of its multiple functions and numerous terminal connections the selector switch may appear complex. Your circuit diagram will help you isolate only the contacts that may be part of your problem, and the ohmmeter can quickly determine if a problem exists.

Note: Gaining access to the oven selector switch will vary depending upon your range model type. However, the inspection and repair steps are similar for free-standing, hi/low, built-in and wall ovens. For example purposes, Procedure 22 will only explain how to test and replace oven selector switches found on free-standing ranges.

Oven selector switch

Step 1: Be sure all range controls are turned **OFF**. Disconnect the power supply at the distribution panel and unplug the range from the receptacle. Watch for sharp edges.

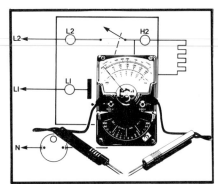

Step 2: This procedure requires the use of an ohmmeter and the ability to read a circuit diagram. For instructions please refer to Tools and Testing Equipment, pages 96-98.

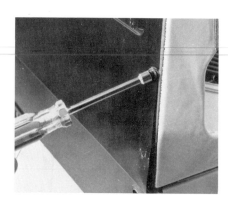

Step 3: This procedure requires the removal of access panels from your range. If you are unfamiliar with this process, please refer to Procedure #3: Removing Access and Control Panels.

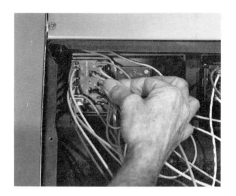

Step 4: To visually inspect selector switch, remove top access panel. Inspect terminals carefully for oxidation or discoloring. Replace switch if overheating is evident.

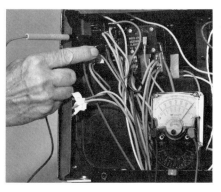

Step 5: With switch still attached to range, use ohmmeter to check electrical continuity of switch. Set meter to R x 1 scale and check across each set of contacts while turning selector switch to various positions. Meter needle should sweep to zero ohms if contact is good.

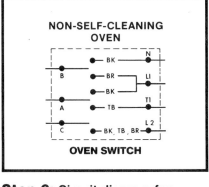

Step 6: Circuit diagram for typical non-self-cleaning oven. With ohmmeter at R x 1, test contacts which should be closed at each switch position. Meter should read zero ohms. Example: At BAKE, contacts L1 and A; N and B; and L2 and C should be closed.

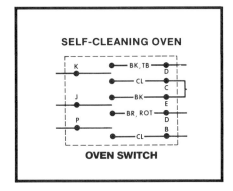

Step 7: This circuit diagram is for a typical self-cleaning oven. With ohmmeter at R x 1, test contacts which should be closed at each switch position. Meter should read zero ohms. Example: at BAKE, contacts K and D; and J and E should be closed.

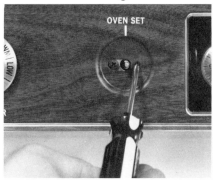

Step 8: To remove selector switch pull switch knob off the shaft and loosen the two screws holding switch to control panel.

Step 9: Accessing switch from rear of range, pull switch free of control panel.

Step 10: Grasp wire at its terminal and remove from switch terminal. (For installation reference make note of how wires are connected.)

Step 11: To install new switch, attach wiring in original position. Firmly attach push-on terminals. Secure switch mounting screws for proper grounding.

23 Range body cosmetics

Skill Level Rating:

Easy	Average	Difficult	Very Difficult

Some of the problems you encounter with your range may deal with cosmetic repairs. Such repairs include replacing a damaged cabinet panel, or touching up a scratch. Cooktop surface and oven doors are finished with a porcelain enamel and are difficult to repair. The recommended procedure is to replace the damaged panel.

Most bodies and drawer fronts have a painted surface. Matching touch-up paint is available in aerosol cans and touch-up pencils. Trim, handles, and range body parts for recent model ranges can be ordered through your local appliance parts dealer.

Step 1: Be sure all range controls are turned **OFF**. Disconnect the power supply at the distribution panel and unplug the range from the receptacle. Watch for sharp edges. Apply paint only in well-ventilated area.

Step 2: Damaged trim is replaced by removing retaining screws or clips, removing damaged trim and installing new one. To avoid chipping, use care not to overtighten screws that attach trim to porcelain panel.

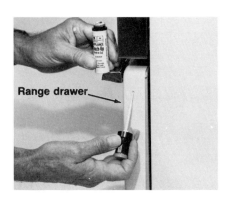

Range drawer

Step 3: To repair small paint scratches, spray small amount of paint into top of can and dip torn end of paper match in paint or use touch-up pencil. Using paint sparingly, fill scratch. Use several coats to avoid runs.

Step 4: Large scratches with deep edges should be sanded smooth with extra fine sand paper. Sand until edge is "feathered" smoothly into exposed metal. Follow painting instructions on paint can.

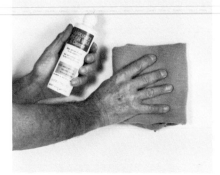

Step 5: To blend repair into panel, wax with appliance polish. Use care not to allow wax to come into contact with door gasket or plastic surface.

24 Adjusting the oven thermostat

Skill Level Rating:	Easy	**Average**	Difficult	Very Difficult

Oven thermostats are factory calibrated when your oven is manufactured and normally require no further adjustment. Critical calibration is possible only by using a special thermocouple-type thermometer.

Sometimes, slight shifts in calibration occur with age. You may notice this if a favorite recipe takes too long to bake. You can compensate for slight shift by making minor adjustments that do not require the removal of the thermostat.

If the temperature level of the thermostat changes suddenly or continues to drift after you make a calibration, an internal problem has occurred, and the thermostat should be replaced.

Oven temperature switch

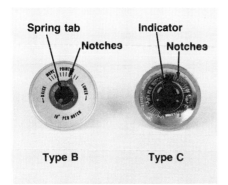

Step 1: Be sure all range controls are turned **OFF.** Disconnect the power supply at the distribution panel and unplug the range from the receptacle. Watch for sharp edges.

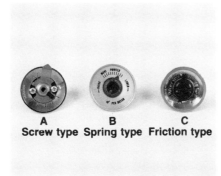

A — Screw type   B — Spring type   C — Friction type

Step 2: Remove oven temperature control knob by pulling straight off. Look at back of knob. It will be one of three types: A) with two retaining screws, B) with a spring clip tab, or C) with friction fitting.

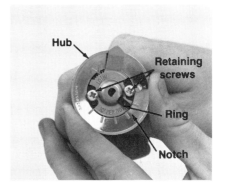

Hub, Retaining screws, Ring, Notch

Step 3: For control knob type A. Loosen retaining screws and move ring one notch, as indicated by arrows on hub, to increase or decrease temperature by 10 degrees. Move only one notch at a time, until oven is performing properly. Tighten retaining screws and replace knob.

Spring tab   Indicator   Notches   Notches

Type B   Type C

Step 4: For knob types B and C. Hold the outer ring and turn the knob so spring tab or indicator moves one notch, as indicated by arrows, to increase or decrease temperature by 10 degrees. Move only one notch at a time, until oven is performing properly. Replace knob.

25 Inspecting and replacing oven thermostat (non-self-cleaning)

Skill Level Rating:	Easy	Average	**Difficult**	Very Difficult

The temperature in non-self-cleaning ovens is controlled by the oven thermostat, a sealed capillary tube sensing device that runs from a switch behind the temperature selector knob to a mounting inside the oven.

Inside the capillary tube is a material that expands as the heat increases. The contacts that energize the heating unit are operated by a bellows that enlarges with the expanding material. As the oven cools, the bellows collapses, allowing the contacts to retouch and energize the heating unit.

The distance between the bellows and the contacts is controlled by the setting on the temperature control knob. The closer the bellows is to the contacts, the lower the oven temperature. If the oven temperature is too high or low, the oven thermostat may simply need calibrating as described in Procedure 24: Adjusting the Oven Thermostat.

IMPORTANT: The capillary tube must be handled with care. Repeated bending or very sharp bends could cause the tube to rupture. This defect results in high heat at all oven settings and demands thermostat be replaced.

Oven thermostat (behind oven temperature control knob)

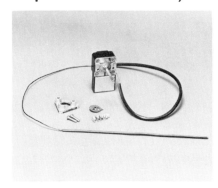

Thermostat replacement kit

Step 1: Be sure all range controls are turned **OFF.** Disconnect the power supply at the distribution panel and unplug the range from the receptacle. Watch for sharp edges. Be especially careful when handling thermostat capillary tube.

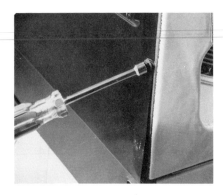

Step 2: This procedure requires removal of access panels from your range. If you are unfamiliar with this process, please refer to Procedure #3: Removing Access and Control Panels.

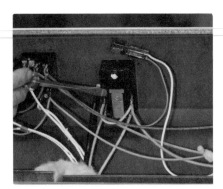

Step 3: Oven thermostat is located behind oven temperature control knob. Remove panel which gives access to thermostat. Inspect terminals for discoloration or burned material around terminals. Replace thermostat if damaged.

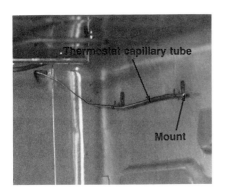

Step 4: To replace thermostat, follow thermostat capillary tube from entry into oven cavity to its mounting support. Gently free capillary tube from mounting support.

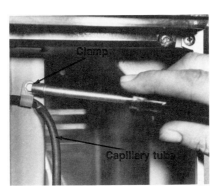

Step 5: Capillary tube can be reached after access panel is removed. Look for clamps positioned around tube. If present, remove before pulling tube from oven.

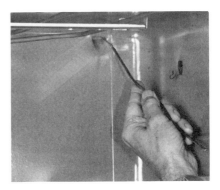

Step 6: With tube free of mounting supports and clamps, push gently through oven wall. Handle capillary tube with care at all times.

Step 7: Pull oven temperature control knob off shaft. Remove screws that hold thermostat to backsplash or control panel.

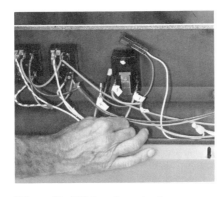

Step 8: Wiring terminals may now be disconnected from back of thermostat. (For installation reference, make note of how wires are connected.)

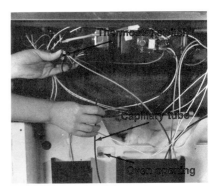

Step 9: Gently lift out thermostat. Carefully follow instructions that come with new thermostat.

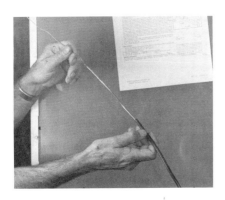

Step 10: To install new thermostat, be careful that capillary tube is routed away from electrical terminals. Transfer any insulating tubing from old to new thermostat, securing as on old thermostat.

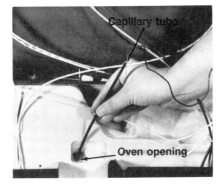

Step 11: Feed capillary tube back through oven wall and remount to inside support. Attach thermostat to control panel, replacing all wiring terminals in original position.

Step 12: When replacing knob to front of control panel, check and reset calibration indicator to center position as described in Procedure #24: Adjusting the Oven Thermostat.

26 Inspecting and replacing clock timer

Skill Level Rating: | Easy | Average | **Difficult** | Very Difficult |

The timer on your range serves a dual purpose. It is a clock, and it can be set to turn the oven on and off at a pre-set interval. On some range models, the clock timer may control a timed receptacle, which can be used for such chores as turning on a coffeemaker before you get up in the morning.

The timer is divided into two sections, the motor and gear train for the clock mechanism, and contact switches which control the electrical function. Each section is tested independently. Close observation of the timer in operation can tell you which section of the timer is causing the problem. The timer can usually be tested in place. However, it must be removed for replacement or cleaning.

Clock timer

Note: The clock timer on your range may not appear the same as the one above. The steps in this procedure, however, can be used on all range timers.

Step 1: Be sure all range controls are turned **OFF**. Disconnect the power supply at the distribution panel and unplug the range from the receptacle. Watch for sharp edges on control panel and timer parts.

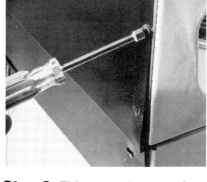

Step 2: This procedure requires the removal of access and/or control panels from your range. To gain access to the timer, follow the appropriate steps for your model in Procedure #3: Removing Access and Control Panels.

Step 3: If clock does not run, check fuse in range. (See Procedure #28). If fuse is all right yet timer functions are inoperative, replace complete timer.

Step 4: To remove timer for replacement or cleaning, locate and unscrew screws that mount timer to backsplash or control panel. Disconnect wires. (For installation reference, make note of how wires are connected.)

Step 5: Once timer is removed, backside of clock's glass may be cleaned. Use extreme caution to keep cleaning cloth and solution from contacting wiring or other components.

Step 6: Handle glass carefully. Clean with warm water and liquid dishwashing detergent. With dry cloth only brush away any food particles that may have collected on clock face.

Step 7: To replace timer, mount timer in original position. Be sure wires are attached correctly.

27 Inspecting and replacing range lights

Skill Level Rating:	Easy	Average	**Difficult**	Very Difficult

Range lights operate on a 120-volt circuit within the range. The oven light is a special 40-watt appliance bulb designed to withstand high oven temperatures. The oven light is operated by the opening and closing of the oven door. In addition, doors with windows have a special external switch to turn the light on for viewing food without opening the oven door.

Cooktop lights are fluorescent tubes operated by a switch on the control panel. Types of installation may vary with different range models. Details of light replacement are covered in each model's *Use and Care Book*.

Oven light

Oven light

Cooktop light

Step 1: Be sure all range controls are turned **OFF**. Disconnect the power supply at the distribution panel and unplug the range from the receptacle. Watch for sharp edges.

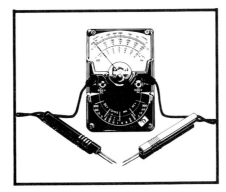

Step 2: This procedure requires the use of an ohmmeter. For instructions, please refer to Tools and Testing Equipment, page 96.

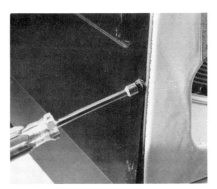

Step 3: This procedure requires removal of access panels from your range. If you are unfamiliar with this process, please refer to Procedure #3: Removing Access and Control Panels.

Step 4: <u>Oven light</u>. When the oven light fails to operate, first check the bulb. Pull down wire bail or remove screws to free glass shield. Replace a burnt-out bulb with a new 40-watt, heat-resistant appliance bulb.

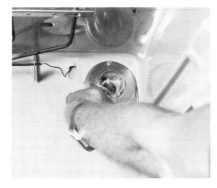

Step 5: If you do not have a 40-watt appliance bulb on hand, test the socket by screwing in an ordinary light bulb. If bulb lights, remove immediately and replace with 40-watt appliance bulb. If not, test switch. Do not leave ordinary light bulb in oven.

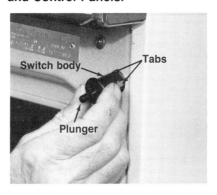

Step 6: To remove switch, carefully insert edge of small screwdriver under flange of switch, depress release tabs and rock switch gently out through opening.

Step 7: With ohmmeter set at R x 1, place probes on switch terminals. Needle should sweep to 0 ohms. Depress switch plunger and needle should fall. If switch tests good, go to Step 9; if not, replace switch.

Step 8: To replace oven light switch, disconnect two wire leads from old switch. Connect leads to same terminals on new switch. Insert switch in opening and snap into position.

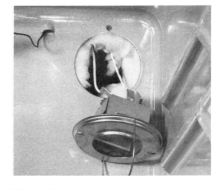

Step 9: Inspect light socket. On non-self-clean ranges, socket terminals are accessible from inside oven. Remove glass shield and screws holding light assembly in place and pull assembly out into oven for inspection.

27 continued

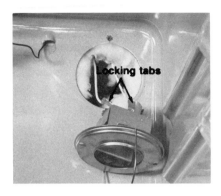

Step 10: Inspect for signs of damage. If socket is damaged, remove by squeezing locking tabs. Push out old socket and replace with new one.

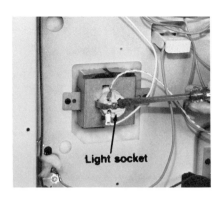

Step 11: On free-standing self-clean ranges, oven light socket is accessible only from rear of range. Remove rear access panel and inspect light receptacle for damage. Area not accessible on built-in ranges or wall ovens (call service technician).

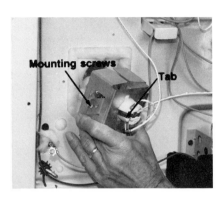

Step 12: To replace damaged socket, remove mounting screws and lift out assembly. Compress tabs and push out damaged socket. Insert new socket.

Step 13: <u>Fluorescent cooktop light.</u> If fluorescent cooktop light burns out or shows large blackened areas, it must be replaced. Follow instructions in your range's *Use & Care Book*.

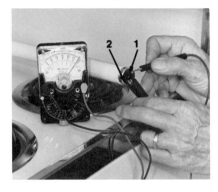

Step 14: To test fluorescent tube, set ohmmeter to R x 1. Test terminals 1 and 2. Needle should sweep upscale. Repeat test at other end. If either test fails, replace tube.

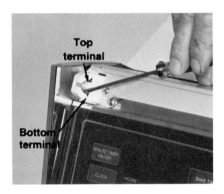

Step 15: If lamp tests properly, check light sockets to assure proper contact with lamp pins. Terminals should exert simultaneous contact with tube pins.

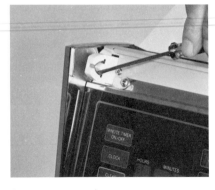

Step 16: If terminal is sprung, it may be gently bent back into position using longnose pliers or screwdriver.

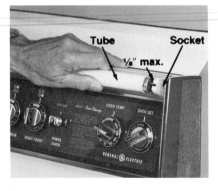

Step 17: Gap between tube and sockets should be no more than 1/8-inch. If sockets have been bent outward, gently bend back into position. If tube and sockets show no damage, check fluorescent light switch.

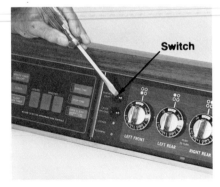

Step 18: Fluorescent light switch is located on the backsplash of free-standing ranges, behind backsplash rear access panel; on Hi/Low models, at bottom of control panel. For access, open control panel.

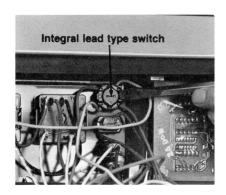

Step 19: To test switch, find momentary contact leads that lead to lamp receptacle. On switch with push-on terminals, these leads have red marks. On integral lead switch (pictured above) there are no identifying marks.

Step 20: If you cannot remove leads from switch, insert straight pin through center of each lead for attachment of ohmmeter probes. With ohmmeter set at R x 1, depress and fold in switch button. Needle should sweep to 0 ohms. Remove pins.

Step 21: Test other two leads the same way, only this time depress and release switch button without holding in. Needle should sweep to 0 ohms only when switch is in "ON" position. If both tests are good, go to Step 23; if not, replace switch

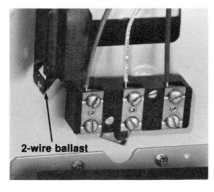

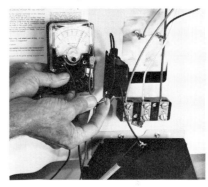

Step 22: To replace switch, unscrew knurled ring that holds switch to range body. (For installation reference, make note of how wires are connected.) Cut leads near switch and install new switch, using ceramic wire nuts.

Step 23: If lamp and switch are functioning, check ballast. The ballast may be a 2-wire or 3-wire type, located in the control panel area or on back of range body.

Step 24: To check 2-wire ballast, disconnect leads at easiest access point. On some ranges, leads may have to be cut and spliced. Connect ohmmeter to leads and set to R x 1. Meter should read about 15 to 25 ohms.

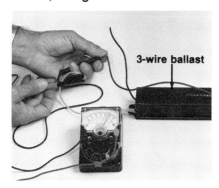

Step 25: To check 3-wire ballast, disconnect blue and white leads (cut and splice). Connect ohmmeter to leads and set to R x 1. Meter should read about 50 to 60 ohms.

Step 26: If tests fail, replace ballast. (For installation reference, make note of how wires are connected.) If leads are cut, strip insulation and reconnect with ceramic high-temperature wire nut.

28 Inspecting and replacing appliance receptacles

Skill Level Rating:	Easy	**Average**	Difficult	Very Difficult

Electrical receptacles (outlets) are provided on the backsplash or control panel of some ranges to plug in other appliances, e.g., a coffeepot or mixer. These receptacles operate on a 110-volt circuit, and some are connected to the range timer for turning an appliance on at a specific time.

Since plugged-in appliances can draw excess current, an internal type "S" fuse keeps the circuit from overloading and damaging range wiring.

Appliance receptacles

28 continued

Step 1: Be sure all range controls are turned **OFF**. Disconnect the power supply at the distribution panel and unplug the range from the receptacle. Watch for sharp edges.

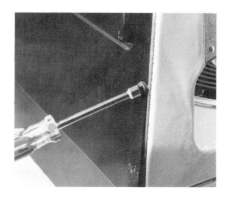

Step 2: This procedure requires removal of access panels from your range. If you are unfamiliar with this process, please refer to Procedure #3: Removing Access and Control Panels.

Step 3: If appliance receptacle is timed type, be sure timer has been properly set. See your *Use and Care Book*. If receptacle still fails to operate, or if it is the non-timed type, check fuse.

Step 4: On most ranges, fuse is located under cooktop at left rear. It can be reached through the left rear surface unit opening. On some built-in ranges, it is next to right front surface unit.

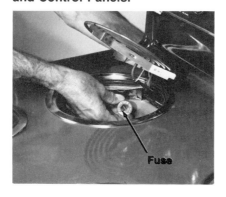

Step 5: Replace blown fuse with another of the same rating and type. If fuse has metal cover, be sure to replace it.

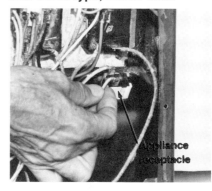

Step 6: Remove access panel or control panel and inspect wiring terminals for appliance receptacle. Tighten any loose connections. Check that connections are clean, with no burned-off wires, discoloration or charred material around terminals.

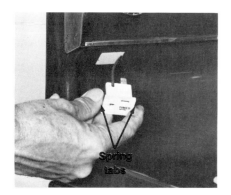

Step 7: To remove damaged receptacle, disconnect wiring leads. (For installation reference, make note of how wires are connected.) Depress spring tabs and push receptacle through front of range.

Step 8: To install new appliance receptacle, snap socket into place. Connect gray or white wire to silver-colored terminal. Connect black or red wire to brass-colored terminal. Connect green ground lead to range.

29 Inspecting and replacing self-cleaning oven sensor

Skill Level Rating:	Easy	Average	**Difficult**	Very Difficult

Some self-cleaning ovens use a sensor as part of their solid-state control circuit. If your self-cleaning oven has a temperature control knob with mechanical "stops" at the WARM and BROIL settings, you will find a sensor mounted on inside rear oven wall near the top left corner.

This type of sensor is a resistor which increases in resistance in proportion to the temperature inside the oven. This change in resistance signals the printed circuit (PC) board control to provide the proper temperature level for effective oven cleaning or baking. If the sensor fails, the oven will not operate.

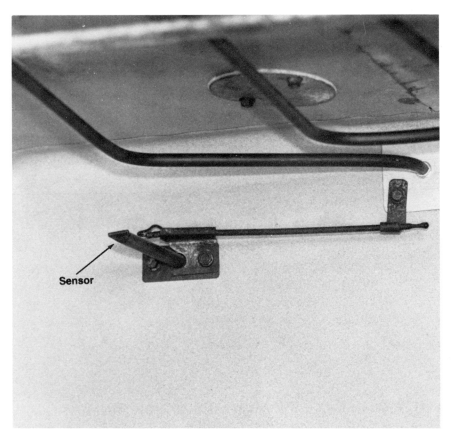

Sensor

Self-cleaning oven sensor

Step 1: Be sure all range controls are turned **OFF**. Disconnect the power supply at the distribution panel and unplug the range from the receptacle. Watch for sharp edges.

Step 2: This procedure requires the use of an ohmmeter. For instructions on how to use an ohmmeter, please refer to Tools and Testing Equipment, page 96.

Step 3: This procedure requires the removal of access panels from your range. If you are unfamiliar with this process, please refer to Procedure #3: Removing Access and Control Panels.

75

Step 4: Locate printed circuit board. On free-standing and built-in ranges, as well as wall ovens, PC board is located behind control panel. On Hi/Low ranges, PC board is behind fluorescent light.

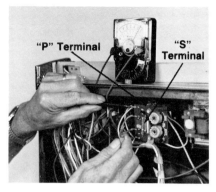

Step 5: Remove lead from "S" terminal on PC board. Set ohmmeter to R x 1 and test from removed "S" lead to terminal "P" on board. Needle should move partially upscale. If test fails, replace oven sensor.

Step 6: If you can access the backside of your oven, remove rear access panel and locate where the sensor wires enter the oven. Cut sensor leads close to oven opening. Position range leads for easy access later.

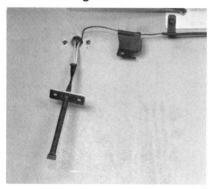

Step 7: If you cannot work easily from the rear, you can replace sensor from inside your oven, provided the opening is at least ½ inch. If the opening is smaller, the wire connectors will not fit through. You will have to pull oven from wall (a 2-person job) to service from rear.

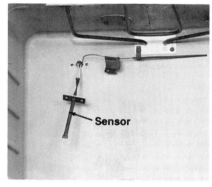

Step 8: Remove the two mounting screws on the sensor bracket inside the oven. If leads were not cut from rear, pull leads into oven and cut them close to sensor. Remove sensor from oven.

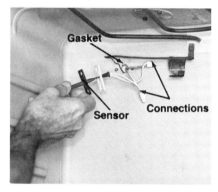

Step 9: Strip insulation from sensor and range leads to expose ½" of bare wire. Twist range leads and sensor leads together, then cap with ceramic wire nuts that came with new sensor. Ordinary wire nuts melt and should not be used in oven.

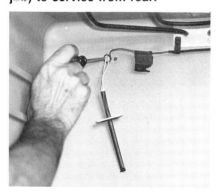

Step 10: If working from inside the oven, guide sensor leads and connectors one at a time through oven opening. Using a small, long screwdriver, make sure all excess wire and wire nuts extend through oven insulation to back of range.

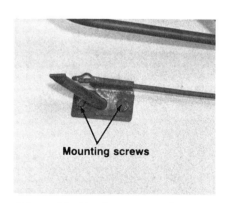

Step 11: Replace mounting screws to secure sensor in oven.

30 Inspecting and replacing self-cleaning oven transformer

Skill Level Rating:	Easy	Average	Difficult	**Very Difficult**

On self-cleaning ranges with solid-state control systems, a step-down transformer is used to provide approximately 12 volts to the control circuit. These models can be identified by having mechanical "stops" at the BROIL and WARM positions on the oven temperature control knob. If the transformer fails to furnish power to the control circuit, the oven will not operate.

There are two separate coils of wire inside the transformer. When 120-volt power is fed into one of the coils (primary winding), it sets up a magnetic field which creates 12 volts in the other coil (secondary winding).

Self-cleaning oven transformer

Step 1: Be sure all range controls are turned **OFF**. Disconnect the power supply at the distribution panel and unplug the range from the receptacle. Watch for sharp edges.

Step 2: This procedure requires the use of an ohmmeter. For instructions, please refer to Tools and Testing Equipment, page 96.

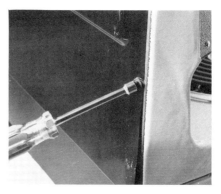

Step 3: This procedure requires removal of access panels from your range. If you are unfamiliar with this process, please refer to Procedure #3: Removing Access and Control Panels.

Step 4: Locate transformer. On wall ovens, it is behind control panel. On free-standing and built-in ranges, it is behind control panel or on back of range. Transformer in Hi/Low models is inside control compartment or on range back.

Step 5: Some ranges have transformers for different purposes. Trace leads to ensure testing of correct transformer. Self-cleaning transformer has one of its leads connected to the PC board.

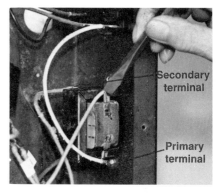

Step 6: Transformer can be tested with ohmmeter for continuity through each of the two windings. Primary winding is usually marked "P" and has larger terminals. Secondary winding is usually marked "S" and has smaller terminals.

Step 7: Set ohmmeter to R x 1. Disconnect one primary lead and test across primary terminals. Repeat for secondary terminals. Needle should move for both tests.

Step 8: If either test fails, replace transformer. Remove mounting screws and wire leads. (For installation reference, make note of how wires are connected.) Install new transformer.

31 Inspecting and replacing high temperature limit switch

Skill Level Rating:	Easy	Average	Difficult	**Very Difficult**

If your self-cleaning range has mechanical "stops" at the BROIL and WARM positions on the oven temperature control knob, your oven has a high temperature limit switch. This switch serves two functions. It provides protection against excessive temperatures during the bake cycle. It also locks the door during the clean cycle.

Caution: Use extreme care when handling capillary tube and bulb. Wear goggles and gloves. Do not bend excessively or repeatedly. Contents of capillary bulb and tube (sodium and potassium hydroxide) produce lye in the presence of moisture. If contents contact skin, remove all material with a DRY towel or cloth (NEVER USE WATER). Then wash area thoroughly with mild soap and water. If assembly ruptures, crimp broken ends with pliers.

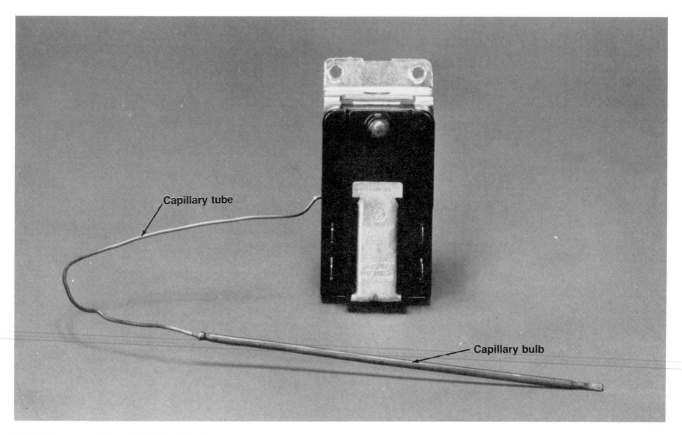

High temperature limit switch

31 continued

Step 1: Be sure all range controls are turned **OFF**. Disconnect the power at the distribution panel and unplug the range. Watch for sharp edges. Wear goggles and gloves when removing and replacing switch.

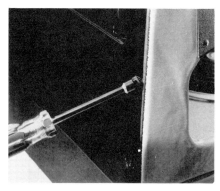

Step 2: This procedure requires the removal of access panels from your range. If you are unfamiliar with this process, please refer to Procedure #3: Removing Access and Control Panels.

Step 3: Locating switch. Switch is found behind rear access panel. Check for damage or loose wires. (On built-in ranges and wall ovens, switch is not accessible, call service technician.)

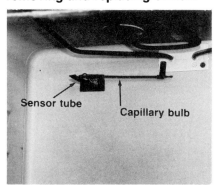

Step 4: Locating capillary bulb. Capillary bulb is found next to sensor tube in oven. Check for damage. If capillary bulb or tube is damaged, do not handle without gloves and goggles.

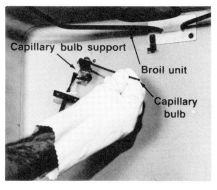

Step 5: If switch, tube or bulb is damaged or malfunctioning, replace entire unit. Wear gloves and goggles. Carefully remove capillary bulb from mounting bracket. Remove mounting screws from capillary bulb support. Pull sensor into oven but do not disconnect.

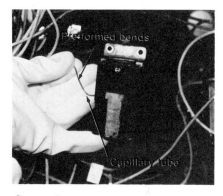

Step 6: From rear of range remove switch. (For installation reference, make note of how wires are connected.) Carefully remove entire assembly. Do not sharply bend capillary tube. Dispose of properly as instructed on new switch package.

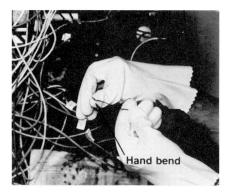

Step 7: Reverse above procedure to install new switch assembly. Be sure to maintain pre-formed bends. Carefully hand-bend tube as needed to fit as shown in Step 6.

32 Inspecting, adjusting and replacing solid-state oven temperature control

Skill Level Rating:	Easy	Average	**Difficult**	Very Difficult

If your self-cleaning oven has mechanical "stops" at WARM and BROIL on the oven temperature control knob, it has a solid-state control system. Turning the temperature control knob adjusts a variable resistor behind the knob, and the temperature of the oven determines the resistance of the oven sensor.

A bias resistor built into the printed circuit board (PC board) allows the oven temperature to go up to 880 degrees during the self-clean cycle. If absolutely necessary, the clean temperature can be adjusted at the circuit board. This would be done in cases of insufficient or partial cleaning due to too low a clean cycle temperature. This adjustment should be made only after all other suggested procedures have failed to correct the problem. High temperature pellets are available for testing the cleaning temperature.

NOTE: Do not adjust bake temperature at printed circuit board. Bake temperature should only be adjusted at temperature control knob. (See Procedure #24.)

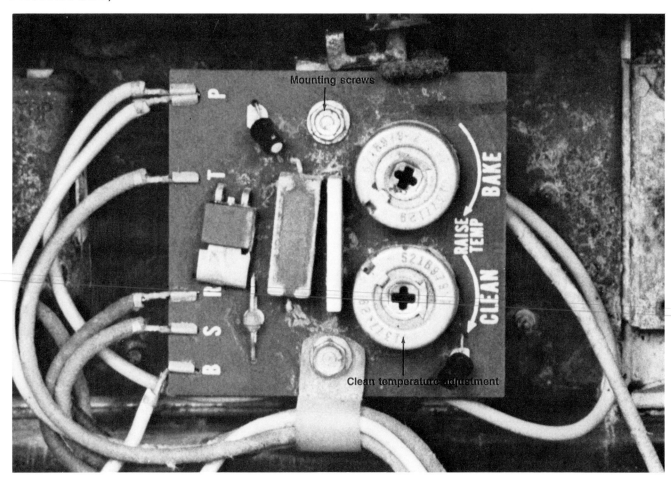

Solid-state oven temperature control (PC board)

32 continued

Step 1: Be sure all range controls are turned **OFF**. Disconnect the power supply at the distribution panel and unplug the range from the receptacle. Watch for sharp edges.

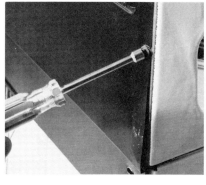

Step 2: This procedure requires the removal of access panels from your range. If you are unfamiliar with this process, please refer to Procedure #3: Removing Access and Control Panels.

Step 3: Use self-clean pellet test to determine if oven is reaching cleaning temperature. Follow instructions on box. If temperature is correct, pellet will melt or change shape, color, and lose 850 markings.

Printed circuit board

Step 4: Locate printed circuit board. On free-standing and built-in ranges, as well as wall ovens, PC board is located behind control panel. On Hi/Low ranges, PC board is behind fluorescent light.

Step 5: Visually inspect printed circuit board for damage, such as burned connectors. Check terminals to be sure they are tight. If any are loose, crimp with pliers and re-test oven with new pellet.

Step 6: Adjust clean temperature only if pellet test indicates too low a temperature. Use Phillips screwdriver to adjust self-clean temperature slightly by rotating control ⅛ turn in desired direction. If necessary, repeat test.

Step 7: Replace PC board if damaged or adjustment unsuccessful. Remove mounting screws and wires. (For installation reference, make note of how wires are connected.) Be sure fiber washers are properly installed.

33 Inspecting and replacing hot wire relay

Skill Level Rating:	Easy	Average	**Difficult**	Very Difficult

On some self-cleaning ovens, a hot wire relay is used to cycle oven heating units on and off during the cleaning cycle. If your self-cleaning oven has a temperature control knob with mechanical "stops" at WARM and BROIL, it has a solid-state control system which uses a hot wire relay.

Inside the relay, a special wire holds contacts open until it is energized by the solid-state control circuit. When the wire is energized, it expands and allows the contacts to close. The closed contacts complete a circuit which energizes the oven heating units.

When a sensor in the oven reaches the preset temperature, it activates the solid-state control circuit. The control circuit then de-energizes the hot wire relay, which opens the contacts again and allows the oven heating units to cycle off.

Hot wire relay

Self-cleaning oven hot wire relay

33 continued

Step 1: Be sure all range controls are turned **OFF**. Disconnect the power at the distribution panel and unplug the range from receptacle. Watch for sharp edges.

Step 2: This procedure requires the use of an ohmmeter. For instructions on how to use an ohmmeter, please refer to Tools and Testing Equipment, page 96.

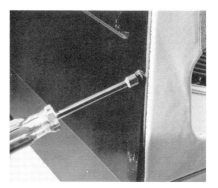

Step 3: This procedure requires the removal of access panels from your range. If you are unfamiliar with the process, please refer to Procedure #3: Removing Access and Control Panels.

Step 4: Locate the hot wire relay on your range. On free-standing, built-in and Hi/Low models, the relay will be found behind the control panel or on the back of range. The hot wire relay is behind the control panel on wall ovens.

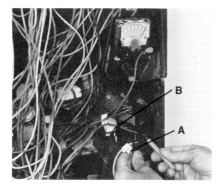

Step 5: To test hot wire relay while in range, set ohmmeter to R x 1. Locate terminals A and B (smallest terminals). Remove lead from one of these terminals and test between A and B. Needle should indicate approximately 5 ohms. If test fails, replace relay.

Step 6: Next, remove lead from terminal 1 or 2 and test these terminals with ohmmeter set to R x 1. Meter needle should not move. Reconnect lead, then repeat test for terminals 3 and 4. Meter needle should not move. If needle moves on either test, replace hot wire relay.

Step 7: To replace hot wire relay, remove leads and mounting screws. (For installation reference, make note of how wires are connected.) Install new relay and reconnect leads.

34 Inspecting and replacing thermal switch

| Skill Level Rating: | Easy | Average | Difficult | **Very Difficult** |

The thermal switch is used in conjunction with the dual range thermostat in some self-cleaning ranges. The thermal switch is designed with a rod inserted inside a sensing tube. When heated, the tube expands faster than the rod. This differential results in a mechanical movement that opens and closes the switch contacts.

The purpose of the thermal switch is to open the circuit to the door-latch solenoid when the oven is in the clean cycle and temperature reaches 600 degrees. It also interrupts the power to the bake and broil heating units during normal operation if temperature exceeds 620 degrees. This protects the oven from overheating. Some self-cleaning ranges have a fan to help keep surface temperatures cool. On those models, the thermal switch energizes the fan when oven temperature is above 530 degrees during the clean cycle.

Thermal switch

Step 1: Be sure all range controls are turned **OFF**. Disconnect the power supply at the distribution panel and unplug the range from the receptacle. Watch for sharp edges. Be especially careful not to bend the thermal switch.

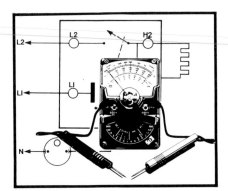

Step 2: This procedure requires the use of an ohmmeter and the ability to read a circuit diagram. For instructions, please refer to Tools and Testing Equipment, pages 96-98.

Step 3: This procedure requires the removal of access panels from your range. If you are unfamiliar with this process, please refer to Procedure #3: Removing Access and Control Panels.

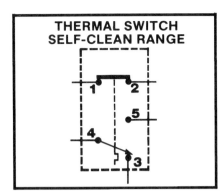

THERMAL SWITCH SELF-CLEAN RANGE

Step 4: The above illustration represents typical circuit diagram for a self-clean range. Markings show settings in which thermal switch contacts should be closed, indicating continuity when checked with ohmmeter.

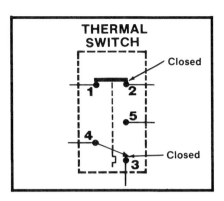

THERMAL SWITCH

Step 5: Circuit diagram shows that contacts 1 and 2 are closed at normal temperatures through oven heating circuit, as are contacts 3 and 4.

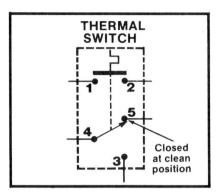

THERMAL SWITCH

Step 6: Contacts 4 and 5 are normally open. At higher temperature these contacts close to energize fan circuit and lock light on models so equipped.

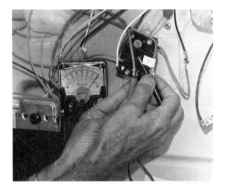

Step 7: Remove bottom rear access panel and locate switch. To test switch, set ohmmeter to R x 1 position and place probes on closed contact terminals, e.g., (1-2) and then (3-4) for diagram above. Needle should sweep upscale to 0 ohms. If test fails, replace switch.

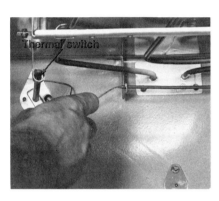

Step 8: Loosen the screws that hold the mounting plates in position from the inside of the oven. The thermal switch extends through this plate and also through a mounting bracket at the front end of the tube.

Step 9: To install new thermal switch, unclip wiring terminals from thermal switch at rear of range. (For installation reference, make note of how wires are connected.)

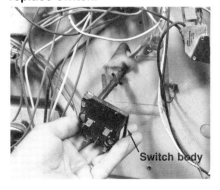

Step 10: To remove switch, rotate switch body about 90 degrees to free tabs from slotted hole in oven liner. Gently pull thermal switch completely out of oven liner.

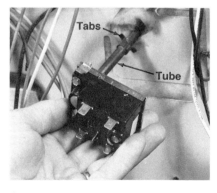

Step 11: Insert new thermal switch into oven liner, making sure to set tabs properly by rotating them 90°. Tube should be away from all thermal switch electrical contacts.

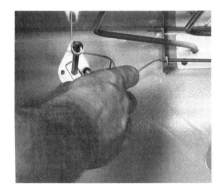

Step 12: Trap capillary tube between gasket and cover plate where it exits from oven cavity. Keep capillary bulb straight. Do not make any sharp bends in capillary tube.

35 Inspecting and replacing dual range thermostat

Skill Level Rating:	Easy	Average	Difficult	**Very Difficult**

The dual range thermostat operates much like the conventional thermostat except that it's designed to operate at the bake and clean temperatures. The following three conditions identify a dual range thermostat: 1) the oven temperature knob has a CLEAN zone and a CLEAN pointer, in addition to the normal temperature setting; 2) a "snap" can be heard and/or felt when the oven temperature knob is rotated all the way clockwise into the CLEAN position; and 3) a thermostat capillary tube is supported in two brackets at the top rear of the oven cavity, below the broil unit.

During normal cooking operations, the dual range thermostat controls the temperature between warm and 550 degrees. When turned to the "clean" position, the contacts are arranged so they maintain the temperature at a level of approximately 880 degrees. A second set of contacts assures that the oven door latch is in the locked position before the clean cycle circuit can be completed. These logic switch contacts prevent oven operation above normal cooking temperatures without the door latch mechanism set for CLEAN.

CAUTION: Use extreme care when handling capillary tube and bulb. Wear goggles and rubber gloves. Do not bend tube excessively or repeatedly. Contents of capillary bulb and tube (sodium and potassium hydroxide) produce lye in the presence of moisture. If contents contact skin, remove all material with a DRY towel or cloth. (NEVER USE WATER.) Then wash area thoroughly with mild soap and water. If assembly ruptures, crimp broken ends with pliers.

Dual range thermostat (behind oven temperature control knob)

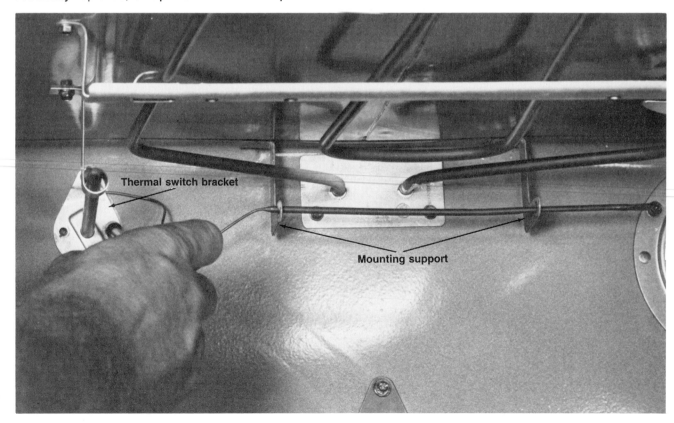

Dual range thermostat controls inside oven cavity

Step 1: Be sure all range controls are turned **OFF**. Disconnect the power supply at the distribution panel and unplug the range from the receptacle. Watch for sharp edges. You will need rubber gloves and goggles to do this procedure.

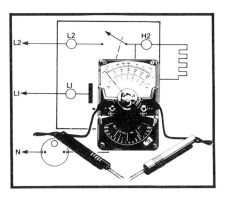

Step 2: This procedure requires the use of an ohmmeter and the ability to read a circuit diagram. For instructions please refer to Tools and Testing Equipment, pages 96-98.

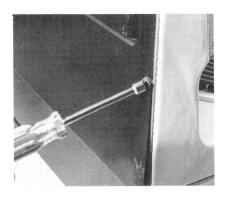

Step 3: This procedure requires the removal of access panels from your range. If you are unfamiliar with this process, please refer to Procedure #3: Removing Access and Control Panels.

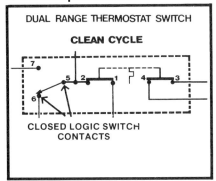

Step 4: Above is a typical circuit diagram for a self-clean range. At settings marked, thermostat logic switch contacts should be closed, with ohmmeter showing continuity.

Step 5: With top rear access panel removed, logic switch can be tested while still in range. Set ohmmeter to R x 1 position to test logic switch contacts 5 and 6 in bake and clean cycles.

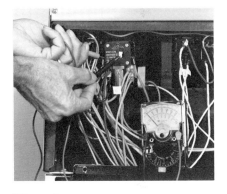

Step 6: Logic switch contacts 5 and 6 should be open when thermostat switch is set to bake, closed when set to clean. When probes are placed across open contacts, needle should not move. If either test fails, replace thermostat.

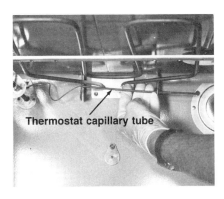

Step 7: To replace thermostat follow thermostat capillary tube from entry into oven cavity to its mounting support. If it's clamped by thermal switch bracket, loosen bracket and pull forward.

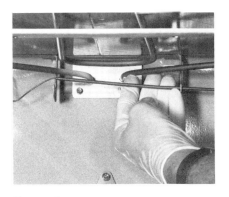

Step 8: Wearing gloves and goggles, free thermostat tube from mounting support.

Step 9: Remove lower rear access panel and look for clamps positioned around tube (such as this one adjacent to thermal switch). Remove all clamps before pulling tube from oven.

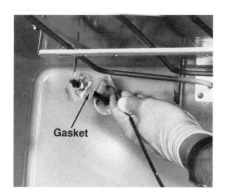

Step 10: With tube free of clamps, tube can now be pushed gently through rear of oven cavity. Use care not to damage gasket at thermal switch bracket.

Step 11: Pull thermostat knob off shaft and remove two screws that hold thermostat to backsplash.

Step 12: Wiring terminals may now be disconnected from back of thermostat. (For installation reference, make note of how wires are connected.)

Step 13: To install new thermostat, be careful that capillary tube is routed away from electrical terminals. Transfer insulating tubing from old to new thermostat, securing as on old thermostat. Wiring terminals must be replaced in original position.

Step 14: Follow carefully instructions that come with new thermostat, disposing of old thermostat as instructed on package. When replacing knob, check and reset calibration indicator in center position.

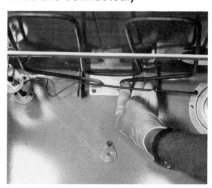

Step 15: Trap capillary tube between gasket and cover plate where it exits from oven cavity. Keep capillary bulb straight. Do not make any sharp bends in capillary tube.

Technical assistance/Service record

This page is provided as a convenient reference for important range repair information. There are spaces for you to record your range model number, parts needed, repair notes (such as where wire leads reattach), and when repairs were made. There are also spaces for you to write down the phone numbers of your nearest GE and Hotpoint parts dealer and Factory Service Center.

Another important phone number for repair information belongs to The GE Answer Center™. If you have difficulty in making any repair described in this book you can contact The GE Answer Center™ by calling 800-626-2000 toll free. The trained service professionals will try to talk you through the problem step. It helps to write down your model number, what you have done, and what is causing you difficulty before calling.

Model number:_____

Parts or components needed:

_____

_____

_____

Repair notes:

_____

_____

_____

Service record:

_____

_____

_____

Phone number of
General Electric and Hotpoint
parts dealer:_____

Phone number of
General Electric and Hotpoint
Factory Service Center:_____

Preventive maintenance

At General Electric, we're committed to your satisfaction--the basic do's and don'ts included in this section are our way of helping you obtain the best results from your General Electric or Hotpoint range. Preventive maintenance is a vital key to long life for your range. The few minutes you invest in caring for your range properly can save you a great deal of time and trouble.

This section outlines basic precautions and simple maintenance routines that will help prevent the small problems that can lead to big repair jobs. Take a little time to read this part of the manual and follow the advice given.

Range exterior maintenance

- Never permit anyone to climb or stand on the range; damage or injury could result.
- When cleaning the range, take care not to get water or other liquids inside where they may cause short circuits.
- Avoid use of scouring powders and abrasive materials which can scratch the surface of the porcelain or metal trim and dull its luster.
- A hot range surface should be allowed to cool before it is cleaned since sudden temperature changes can cause fine hairline cracks in the porcelain surface.
- Certain acid substances, such as fruit juice, marinades and vinegar, should be wiped off as soon as possible to avoid permanent etching of the surface.
- When cleaning glass control panels, take care not to allow water to run down inside the panel; this could cause an electrical hazard.

Range cooktop maintenance
Standard cooktop

- Use flat-bottomed cooking utensils for good heat conduction. Containers with other shapes may shorten the life of the surface unit, distort the coils, or damage the range top.
- Choose utensils made of a material suitable for range top cooking. Some types of enameled ware may melt and fuse to the surface unit under high heats, causing possible damage to surface unit or range top.
- Be sure to match cooking container to size of surface unit. Pans which extend more than an inch beyond the trim ring of the unit can cause heat to build up, discoloring the trim ring, possibly cracking the porcelain enamel of the range top and shortening the life of the surface unit.

- Aluminum reflector pans may be cleaned in a self-cleaning oven. They should be placed upside-down on shelf to prevent warping, and nothing should be placed on top of them during the self-clean cycle.
- Chrome-plated reflector pan/rings from ranges with plug-in surface units should not be cleaned in the oven, or severe discoloration will result.
- Chrome-plated reflector pan/rings should not be covered with foil.
- Aluminum reflector pans may be lined with aluminum foil, but always leave the center open the same size as the opening in the pan.
- Calrod® plug-in units must be properly plugged in and seated securely on the trim ring/pan assembly for even heating and to prevent damage to the unit. To avoid short circuiting unit, do not bend or damage the two plug-in terminals.
- The reflector pan under a plug-in unit should not be lined with aluminum foil. If the foil should come in contact with the receptacle, this could cause a short or fire hazard or damage to the range.
- The removable plug-in surface heating units must not be immersed or soaked, and may not be cleaned in the dishwasher or in the self-cleaning oven. To do so may cause severe damage.
- Grease build-up on the underside of the Calrod® surface heating units should be avoided, since this can lead to corrosion. Excessive spillovers can also cause corrosion and should be wiped off as soon as possible.
- To prevent corrosion avoid getting cleaning materials, particularly chlorine-type compounds, on the coils.
- Never cover an oven vent duct with aluminum foil or any other material.

Glass-ceramic cooktop

- Use appropriate utensils for cooking on a glass-ceramic cooktop. All pots should have flat bottoms to avoid hot spots that can cause damage to the range.
- Never cook foods in aluminum foil trays or wrapped in foil. Foil may melt and become fused to the cooktop, thus causing permanent damage.
- To avoid scratching the cooktop surface, use utensils that are clean and dry, and keep the cooktop itself clean and free of dust or dirt.
- Use of cleaning powders, abrasive pads or harsh chemicals must be avoided to prevent permanent damage to the cooktop surface.
- The cooktop must never be used as a cutting board.
- Use cleaner-conditioner regularly to prevent soil build-up on cooktop.

Range interior maintenance
Self-cleaning ovens

- Aluminum foil must never be placed on the oven shelf or over the broil unit. Damage may result to oven finish.
- Do not use abrasive cleaners that can mar the oven interior. Chemical cleaners and coatings must not be used in a self-cleaning oven; residue from any such cleaner will leave spots or streaks which cannot be removed automatically and may cause permanent scarring of the oven interior.
- The woven gasket around the oven door is vital for a proper oven seal, and must not be cleaned or rubbed. Avoid getting any cleaning materials on this woven fiberglass gasket.

- Do not clean with soap, detergent, abrasive pads, brushes, or commercial oven cleaners. These cleaning agents will damage oven's porous surface.
- To protect the special porous liner from scratches, take care in removing and replacing the bottom panel, inserting shelves, or placing dishes in the oven.

Energy saving tips
- Use cooking utensils of medium weight aluminum, with flat bottoms, straight sides, and tight-fitting covers.
- Cook fresh vegetables, etc., with a minimum amount of water in a covered pan.

- Keep an eye on foods when bringing them quickly to temperature on high heat and reduce heat immediately when cooking temperature is reached. Reduce to lowest setting that will keep food cooking. If time allows, do not start at HIGH.
- Heat only the amount of water needed.
- Turn off unit before you are quite finished and complete the cooking with residual heat.
- Use the right pan size for the surface unit. If the pan is too small, or unit too large energy is wasted.
- Pre-heat the oven only when necessary. Most foods will cook satisfactorily without preheating. If

you find pre-heating is necessary, keep an eye on the indicator light and put food in the oven promptly after the light goes out. Never pre-heat for longer than 10 minutes.
- Avoid frequent door openings during baking and roasting.
- Turn off the oven as the cooking operation is complete.
- Use residual heat in the oven whenever possible to finish cooking or for warming, as with precooked desserts, rolls, etc.
- Cook complete meals, large quantities, instead of one item at a time.

Glass-ceramic cooktop cleaning tips

Problem	Cause	To prevent	To remove
Brown streaks and specks	Cleaning with a sponge or dishcloth that has been used for other kitchen cleaning tasks and may contain soil-laden detergent water.	Use Cleaner-Conditioner only with clean, damp paper towel.	Use a light application of Cleaner-Conditioner with clean, damp paper towel.
Blackened burned-on spots	Spatters or spillovers which contact hot cooking area.	Whenever possible, wipe spatters and food spills as they occur. Select correct heat settings and large enough cookware to eliminate boilovers and spattering.	When area has cooled: Use Cleaner-Conditioner with damp paper towel to remove as much burn-on as possible. Use Cleaner-Conditioner with nonimpregnated plastic nylon pads, such as: Dobie® scouring pad, Skruffy® scouring brush, Tuffy® plastic mesh ball.
	Accidental melting of a plastic film such as a bread bag or similar items.	CAUTION: Be careful to avoid steam burns. Be sure unit is cool before putting these items on cooking surface.	If burn-on persists, CAREFULLY scrape with a single-edge razor blade. Hold blade so edge is completely flat on cooktop and blade is at a 30° angle. CAUTION: Be careful to avoid cutting yourself.
Fine "brown lines" (tiny scratches or abrasions which have collected soil)	Coarse particles (salt, sand, sugar or grit) caught between bottom of cookware and cooktop that are not removed before cooking. Using incorrect cleaning materials.	Normal daily use of Cleaner-Conditioner. In area where there is an abundance of sand or dust, be sure to wipe cooktop before using. Use only cleaning materials recommended in this manual.	Tiny scratches are not removable but can be minimized by continual use of Cleaner-Conditioner. Such scratches do not affect cooking performance.
Metal marking (gray or black marks)	Sliding or scraping metal utensils or oven shelf racks across cooktop.	Do not slide racks or other sharp metal objects across cooktop.	Apply Cleaner-Conditioner with dampened towel to cooled surface.
Pitting or spalling	Boilover of sugar syrup and adherence of sugar syrup to hot cooktop.	Select correct heat setting and large enough cookware to eliminate boilovers and spattering. Watch sugar syrup carefully to avoid boilover.	While unit is still hot, turn to OFF. Take several damp paper towels and wipe hot cooktop immediately. CAUTION: Sugar syrup is very hot, so be careful not to burn yourself. Scrape off remainder of burn with single-edge razor blade while unit is still warm--before cooling down completely. Hold blade so edge is completely flat on cooktop and blade is at a 30° angle. CAUTION: Be careful to avoid cutting yourself.
Hardwater spots (a gray or brown stain that does not seem to be removed using Cleaner-Conditioner)	In cooking, condensation often collects and drips when covers are removed.	Daily use of Cleaner-Conditioner applied with a clean, damp paper towel will help to keep the glass ceramic surface free from hard water.	Mix a small amount of Delete® cleanser with tap water to form a thick, wet paste. Apply this mixture to stain area. Let it stand 45 minutes. Scrub with clean, damp paper towel. After stain is removed: Wipe up remaining paste with damp paper towel. Apply dab of Cleanser-Conditioner and polish with paper towel.

Range cleaning tips

Range part	Cleaning materials	General cleaning instructions
Bake unit and broil unit		Do not clean the bake unit or broil unit. Any soil will burn off when the unit is heated. NOTE: The bake unit is hinged and can be lifted to clean the oven floor. If spillover, residue, or ash accumulates around the bake unit, gently wipe around the unit with warm water.
Broiler pan & rack	Soap and water Soap-filled scouring pad Plastic scouring pad	Drain fat, cool pan and rack slightly. (Do not let soiled pan and rack stand in oven to cool). Sprinkle on detergent. Fill pan with warm water and spread cloth or paper towel over the rack. Let both stand for a few minutes. Wash; scour if necessary. Rinse and dry. OPTION: The broiler pan and rack may also be cleaned in a dishwasher.
Control knobs: range top and oven	Mild soap and water	Pull off knobs. Wash gently but do not soak. Dry and return controls to range making sure to match flat area on the knob and shaft.
Outside glass finish	Soap and water	Wash all glass with cloth dampened in soapy water. Rinse and polish with a dry cloth. If knobs on the control panel are removed, do not allow water to run down inside the surface of glass while cleaning.
Metal, including chrome side trims and trim strips	Soap and water	Wash, rinse, and then polish with a dry cloth. DO NOT USE steel wool, abrasives, ammonia, acids, or commercial oven cleaners which may damage the finish.
Porcelain enamel*	Paper towel Dry cloth Soap and water	Avoid cleaning powders or harsh abrasives which may scratch the enamel. If acids should spill on the range while it is hot, use a dry paper towel or cloth to wipe up right away. When the surface has cooled, wash and rinse. For other spills, such as fat spatterings, etc., wash with soap and water when cooled and then rinse. Polish with a dry cloth.
Inside oven door*	Soap and water	On NON-SELF-CLEANING oven with removable door, clean door with soap and water and dry. DO NOT place door under running water or immerse. Note: Upper-oven door on Hi/Low model is not removable. On SELF-CLEANING oven door, clean only door liner outside the gasket. Do not rub or damage gasket. Avoid getting ANY cleaning materials on gasket.
Oven gasket Silicone rubber (heat resistant)	Soap and water	On ovens so equipped locate when door is open. Clean off soil with sudsy water and rinse thoroughly.
Woven fiberglass	None	Avoid getting ANY cleaning materials on gasket.
Oven liner Non-self-cleaning oven	Soap and water	Cool before cleaning. FOR LIGHT SOIL. Frequent wiping with mild soap and water (particularly after cooking meat) will prolong the time between major cleanings. Rinse thoroughly. NOTE: Soap left on liner causes additional stains when oven in reheated.
	Commercial oven cleaner Soap-filled scouring pad	FOR HEAVY SOIL. Choose a non-abrasive cleaner and follow label instructions, using thin layer of cleaner. Use of rubber gloves is recommended. Wipe or rub lightly on stubborn spots. Rinse well. Wipe off any oven cleaner that gets on thermostat bulb. When rinsing oven after cleaning, also wipe off thermostat bulb, found in back, or on side, near top of oven.
Self-cleaning oven	Soap and water	Cool before cleaning. Frequent wiping with mild soap and water will prolong the time between major cleanings. Be sure to rinse thoroughly. For heavy soiling, use your self-cleaning cycle often.
Oven vent duct	Soap and water	Remove the Oven Vent Duct found under the right rear surface unit. Wash in hot, soapy water and dry and replace correctly. On models with glass-ceramic cooktops, oven vents are holes at rear of cooktop and therefore this procedure does not apply.
Reflector drip pan and rings	Soap and water Stiff-bristled brush Soap-filled scouring pad	Clean as described below or in dishwasher. Aluminum reflector pans and rings on models so equipped may be cleaned in Self-cleaning oven by placing two pans, upside down, on each oven shelf. Chrome-plated reflector pan/rings on models with Plug-In Surface Units, CANNOT BE CLEANED IN SELF-CLEANING OVEN.
Rotisserie Spit, forks, Screws, frame	Soap and water Stiff bristled brush Soap-filled scouring pad	Soak in hot sudsy water; scour to remove cooked-on food, or sauces; wash, dry.
Shelves	Soap and water Soap-filled scouring pad Commercial oven cleaner	FOR HAND CLEANING OF SHELVES FROM NON-SELF-CLEANING OVEN ONLY. any materials mentioned here can be used. Rinse thoroughly to remove all materials after cleaning. Note: Some commercial oven cleaners cause darkening and discoloration. When using for first time, test cleaner on small part of shelf and check for discoloration before completely cleaning. FOR SELF-CLEANING OVENS, shelves can be cleaned with the self-cleaning function in the oven. For heavy soil, clean by hand using any and all materials mentioned and then rinse thoroughly.
Storage drawer	Soap and water	For cleaning, remove drawer by pulling it all the way open, tilt up the front and lift out. Wipe out with damp cloth, or sponge and replace. Never use harsh abrasives or scouring pads.
Calrod® surface unit coils		Spatters and spills burn away when the coils are heated. At the end of a meal, remove all utensils from the Calrod® unit and heat the soiled units at HI. Let the soil burn off about a minute and switch the units to OFF. Avoid getting cleaning materials on the coils. Wipe off any cleaning materials with a damp paper towel before heating the Calrod® unit. DO NOT handle the unit before completely cooled. DO NOT self-clean plug-in units. DO NOT immerse plug-in units in any kind of liquid.
Automatic unit sensor	Water, plastic scouring ball	Keep sensor free from grease or spillovers. Wipe sensor at each cleaning of cooktop. For major spillover: when cool, wipe with damp cloth to soften soil; if necessary use a plastic or nylon scouring ball. Do not use steel wool or other harsh materials. Dry.

*Spillage of marinades, fruit juices, and basting materials containing acids may cause discoloration. Spillovers should be wiped up immediately with a paper towel. When the surface is cool, clean and rinse.

Tools and testing equipment

Tools

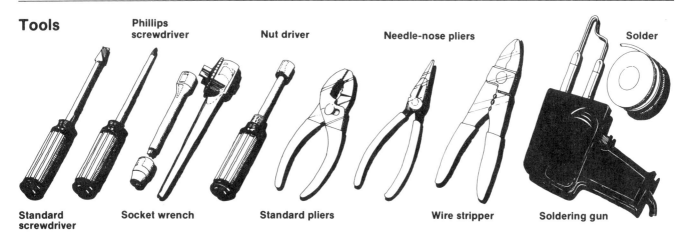

Phillips screwdriver

Nut driver

Needle-nose pliers

Solder

Standard screwdriver

Socket wrench

Standard pliers

Wire stripper

Soldering gun

Chances are you already have some of the above tools in your home. For safety and efficiency reasons it is important to use the proper tools when making range repairs. The tool you will use the most is the screwdriver. Various sizes of standard and Phillips screwdrivers will be necessary to remove the many screws on your range.

Some screws and nuts, especially those used on access panels, have hexagonal heads with no slots. To remove these, you will need either a nutdriver or socket wrench. The nutdriver is made like a screwdriver but has a small socket on one end. This socket fits over the hex head of the screw or nut. It's used just like a screwdriver.

The socket wrench usually has a handle with a ratchet (that can be set to tighten or loosen a nut), an extension and various sockets. Sockets usually come in a set containing several sizes, but the quarter-inch size is most commonly used on the range.

To use a socket wrench, place the socket on the nut and turn the handle counter-clockwise to loosen it. It if makes a clicking sound and does not turn, flip the ratchet lever to the opposite direction and loosen the nut.

You may need soldering equipment to repair loose wiring connections. Use a soldering gun or soldering iron to apply heat at the connection point. Then touch the solder to the heated area and let the solder melt to form a joint. Check with your hardware clerk regarding the best type of soldering supplies for your needs.

Testing equipment

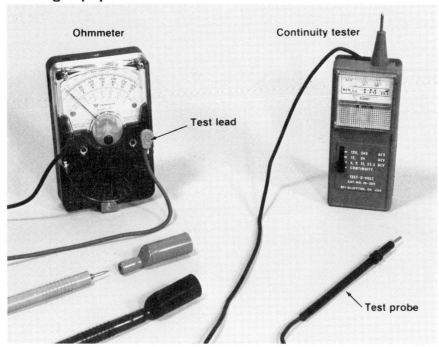

Ohmmeter

Continuity tester

Test lead

Test probe

Either a continuity tester or ohmmeter is required to diagnose the electrical components of your range. The continuity tester is a simple device that indicates the presence of voltage in an electrical circuit. Ohmmeters are usually combined with a voltmeter into an instrument called multimeter, multitester, or volt-ohmmeter (VOM). Volt-ohmmeters have the capability to measure both the presence and amount of voltage in an electrical circuit. A simple inexpensive ohmmeter will be sufficient for any range repairs presented in this manual.

Tools and testing equipment (cont.)

Most problems that occur in an electrical circuit are invisible. For example, it is difficult to see contacts inside a switch that is not closing, or to find a break in the resistance wire inside of a heating unit. For the most part, you'll be using the ohmmeter only as a continuity tester to determine whether or not electrical current can pass through the circuit. By passing a small electrical current from a battery contained inside the ohmmeter through the circuit, you can tell if the circuit is complete.

To understand the basic flow of electricity, think of it in terms of a water pumping station. In order for water to flow through the pipes, it must have a complete "closed loop" from the pump, through the valves, then back to the pump again. If the line is broken or opened at any point, water would eventually cease to flow.

The flow of electricity through your range is similar to the pumping of water, except electrons rather than water are flowing through the range circuitry. The pump is the range plug-in receptacle that provides the force to circulate power through the range circuits. The electrical circuit uses wires rather than pipes as the conductors of electricity and switches rather than valves to control the flow. Voltage is comparable to the pressure that exists in a water circuit, while electrical current could be compared to the flow rate of water that flows through the pipe.

then "zero" the meter by touching the two test probes together. With the probes tightly in contact with each other, the needle of the meter should sweep towards "0" resistance. Now, while holding the probes together, adjust the knob marked "zero adjust" or "ohms adjust" until the needle rests directly over "0".

At this point, you can see exactly how the meter works. If, instead of touching the probes together you touch them to each end of a wire, or to a fuse, the needle should sweep towards 0 (ZERO). This indicates that the wire or fuse will conduct electricity. But if the wire or fuse

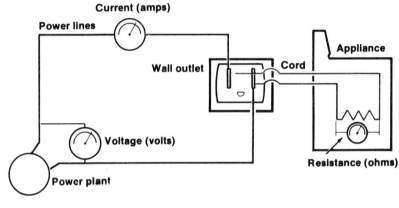

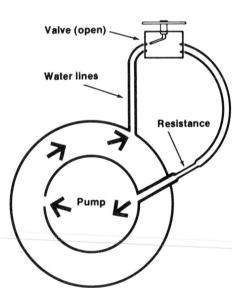

Some tests with an ohmmeter will be needed for repair procedures presented in this manual. An ohmmeter will have either a switch or pair of jacks (plugs) that allow you to select the function of the meter. Resistance is measured in units called ohms and will be designated by the symbol (Ω), or the letter R. Your meter may have more than one range scale. When set at R x 1, the reading should be taken directly from the meter. When set at a higher scale, such as R x 100, the reading on the scale should be multiplied by 100 to obtain the correct resistance. Most measurements for testing components or circuits are made on the lowest scale, usually R x 1.

Plug the test leads in the jacks marked "ohms". The red lead goes in the (+) jack and the black one to (-). If your meter gives you a choice of functions, select the range first,

was broken inside, the needle would not move. When this condition exists in a component or circuit, it is said to be "open" and it cannot conduct electricity. But if the needle moves to indicate that it does conduct electricity, then the component or circuit is said to have "continuity".

All wires in the electrical circuit should indicate 0 (ZERO) resistance when tested in this manner. Switches should indicate 0 (ZERO) resistance when they're turned on, and should be open when turned off. Components that do work such as heating units and transformers will offer some electrical resistance but will not be open. The meter reading for these instances should be somewhere between full scale and no reading.

Many repair procedures in this manual advise you to test for grounds when checking a component. When doing this, you should select the highest resistance scale on the ohmmeter. You will be directed to place one test probe on a terminal of the component and the other test probe on a metallic portion of the component housing. No current should flow through those paths; if the meter indicates that resistance exists under those conditions, the component is grounded and should be replaced.

The repair procedures in this manual will show you the test points (where to place the test probes) for various tests. You'll find the ohmmeter to be a valuable addition to your home tool collection. For further information on the function and operation of an ohmmeter, see pages 94 and 95.

Using the ohmmeter

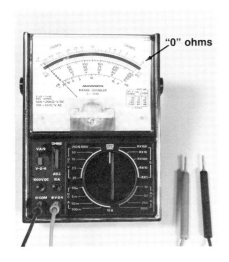

"0" ohms

Full-featured ohmmeter has numerous switch-selected ranges. Note that ohms scale at top is reversed--zero resistance is at full sweep of scale.

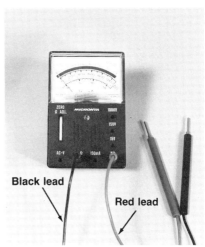

Black lead

Red lead

Inexpensive ohmmeter uses jacks rather than switch to select function; still provides zero ohms adjustment. Note that red lead plugs into positive jack, black into negative or common.

To zero ohmmeter, touch probes tightly together, turn zero adjusting knob until needle is centered over 0 (ZERO) at full sweep of scale. This adjusts readout to the battery condition and to the resistance selected.

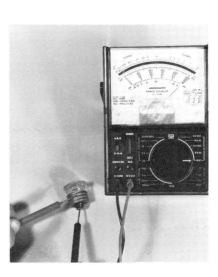

Sometimes you can't see a blown fuse, even when it has a glass shell. Saving a single service call for a simple problem such as this can pay for the price of a meter.

Note: Do not attempt to test resistance of any circuit with the power turned on. Checking a live voltage circuit will damage your testing meter.

Tools and testing equipment (cont.)

How to interpret circuit diagrams

The circuit diagram that accompanies your electric range shows how wiring is connected between components and how the internal electrical circuitry of the components is arranged. The secret to using a circuit diagram as a diagnostic tool is to simplify the diagram. When reading a circuit diagram, focus your attention only on that part of the diagram that involves the area you are testing.

Circuit diagrams may be drawn in several different ways. Some component symbols may be different, but all show the path of current flow from the lines through the switches and components. This flow of current depicts the continuous loop required to complete an electrical circuit.

For explanation purposes, let's study closely the circuit diagram for a four-position standard oven switch circuit (Figure 1). The diagram shows the power supply entering at the left with one 230 volt and two 115 volt circuits available. The two outer lines, identified as L1 (Line 1) and L2 (Line 2), have 230 volts between them. There is 115 volts between L1 and N (Neutral Line) and L2 and N.

Reading the diagram from left to right, we see a wire connected from line N to the Pilot Light and from L1 to 1 (Timer Terminal 1) on the timer switch. When the timer switch is closed (Figure 2), the circuit is completed between timer switch terminal 1 and 2 to terminal T1 on the oven switch.

This oven switch has four positions--OFF, TB (Timed Bake), BK (Bake), and BR (Broil). The diagram (Figure 3) shows how internal switch contacts (enclosed within the box labeled "oven switch") are arranged. Switch positions are indicated on the movable switch arms to show which switches are closed in the various positions. The switch arm

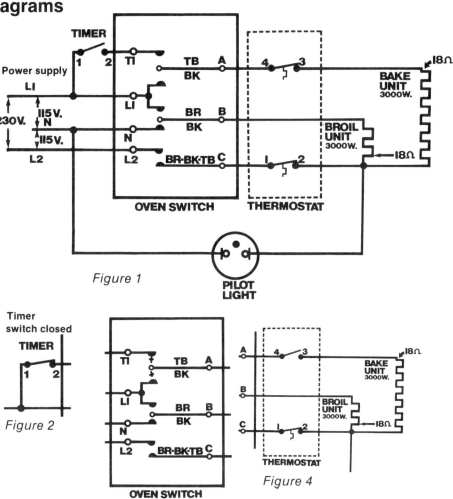

Figure 1

Figure 2

Figure 3

Figure 4

connected to terminal A, for example, moves up to meet contact T1 on the TB (Timed Bake) position and down to meet contact L1 on the BK (Bake) position. Arm B closes to L1 on BR (Broil) and to N on BK (Bake), and arm C closes to L2 on BR (Broil), BK (Bake), and TB (Timed Bake). Referring to the diagram as a guide, you can use your ohmmeter to check the contacts that should be closed in each position. If the contacts do not test closed according to your diagram, the switch should be replaced.

While the oven switch controls the function of the oven, the thermostat reacts to heat in the oven to regulate the temperature level of the oven. The diagram (Figure 4) shows that a wire

connects terminal A of the oven switch to terminal 4 of the thermostat, and terminal C connects to thermostat terminal 1. A wire from terminal 3 of the thermostat connects to one side of the bake unit, represented by the jagged line at the right, whereas a wire from terminal 2 of the thermostat connects to one side of the broil unit and one side of the bake unit. The diagram gives the wattage and resistance of the units, and may also give the color coding of the wires in a particular range. As you can see, both the broil and bake unit of this particular range are 3,000 watt units, that would indicate approximately 18 ohms resistance on an ohmmeter.

97

You can use the diagram to trace the current flow through the circuit at any given position. On the BAKE position (Figure 5), you can follow the circuit from L1 to switch terminal A; through switch 4-3 on the thermostat; then through the bake coil; through thermostat switch terminals 2-1; to oven switch terminal C; and back to L2. With all switches properly closed, this diagram shows that 230 volts should be applied to the bake unit on the BAKE position.

This example of how to read a circuit diagram for a four-position oven switch uses only an excerpt from the complete circuit diagram of a range. By learning to properly interpret circuit diagrams you will have an insight into your range's electrical functions. This in turn should allow you to use your ohmmeter to quickly and accurately pinpoint a problem.

The circuit diagram illustrated in Figures 1-5 represents typical circuitry for a non-self-cleaning range. For specific reference to your range model, check the circuit diagram that came with your range. Circuit diagrams are either glued to the back of the range or located in an envelope behind the control panel. On some new range models, the circuit diagram envelope is glued to the inside of the lower range compartment.

Note: Some of the contacts you will be testing are shown in separate areas on your range circuit diagram. On other diagrams the contacts are marked at various points in the circuit diagram. All contacts are not shown together because they pertain to specific circuits.

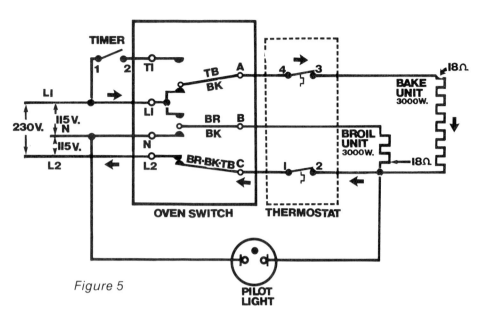

Figure 5

Symbols

The following Legend of Symbols and Abbreviations will assist you in reading the circuit diagrams.

BALLAST		RELAY	
BUZZER		RESISTOR	
FUSE		SOLENOID OR MOTOR WINDING	
HEATING UNIT		SWITCH OR CONTACT	
LAMP - INCANDESCENT		THERMOSTAT	
LAMP - NEON		TRANSFORMER	
MOTOR		WIRES CONNECTED	
OVERLOAD		WIRES CROSSING	
POTENTIOMETER			

Abbreviations

AUTOMATIC
SURFACE UNIT - ASU
BAKE - BK
BROIL - BR
CLEAN - CL
DUAL RANGE
THERMOSTAT - DRT
HOT WIRE RELAY - HWR
POWER - PWR

RELAY - RLY
SMOKE ELIMINATOR - SE
SURFACE UNIT - SU
SWITCH - SW
TIME BAKE - TB
TRANSFORMER - XFMR
WINDING - WDG

Range accessories

In addition to supplying quality original replacement parts for the repair of your range, General Electric also provides a variety of useful range accessories. Some accessories are replacement items that help you keep your range looking and working like new, while others let you add new cooking features to your range. The most popular and widely available range accessories are featured below.

Appliance paint

High quality paints in spray cans and touch-up applicators are available in five colors to match GE/Hotpoint appliances. Camouflaging most nicks and scratches, GE appliance paint is an easy-to-use and long-lasting way to improve your range appearance.

Appliance wax and cleaner

Protective liquid wax contains silicone sealant to clean, polish, and wax in one easy step. The 8-oz. squeeze bottle contains enough liquid wax for several applications to keep your range finish in like-new condition.

WR97X216

Ceramic cooktop cleaner

While designed to remove problem stains on ceramic range cooktops, this mild, abrasive cleaner also works well on copper, tile, brass, porcelain, chrome, and plastic. It comes in a convenient 12 oz. shaker can.

WB10X7

Ceramic cooktop cleaner conditioner

Cleaner is specifically designed for glass range tops and comes in easy-to-use 8 oz. squeeze bottle. Cleans typical cooktop stains and spills while conditioning cooktop surface.

WB64X5020

Light bulbs

Replacement lights for your range are also available from General Electric. Both the oven light (pictured above) and fluorescent cooktop lights are supplied according to electrical specifications for GE/Hotpoint ranges and install easily. The oven light is specifically designed to withstand hot oven temperatures.

Range hood filters

General Electric supplies a variety of range hood filters to fit your range. Shown here are a rectangular activated charcoal filter that helps trap odors as well as grease, and a rounded metal mesh filter. Both snap in for easy installation and protect fan motor from grease build-up.

Drip pans and rings

Drip pans and trim rings collect many food spills over the life of a range and may at some point need replacing. Dramatically improving range appearance, new GE drip pans and trim rings come in several types and sizes to fit your range and budget.

Porcelain drip pans

General Electric also supplies porcelain drip pans that can be cleaned in your self-clean oven. Available for plug-in type surface units, these drip pans also wipe clean easily between major cleanings.

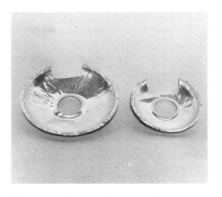

Disposable foil pan liners

If you don't like cleaning drip pans at all, General Electric provides disposable foil drip pan liners. Preformed to provide maximum protection for permanent drip pans, foil liners come in 6″ and 8″ sizes in economical packages of eight liners.

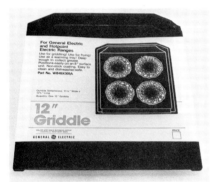

Non-stick griddle

The General Electric griddle fits over most 8″ surface units and comes in a convenient 12″ size. Ideal for grilling, frying, or use as a warming tray, a griddle can add new variety to your range cooking. Deep trough at the griddle base collects drippings.

WB49X305

Family size broiler pan and rack

Original replacement part for broiler pan and rack that comes with most ranges, this set features deep well porcelain-enameled pan and chrome-plated slotted broiler rack. Ideal for calorie- and fat-conscious cooking, the broiler pan keeps fat drippings away from meat.

Broiler rack   WB48X5002
Broiler pan   WB49X88

Small broiler pan and rack

General Electric also provides a smaller size broiler pan and rack that is ideal for smaller portions and households. Having all the features of the larger broiler pan and rack, this smaller size is easy to handle and fit into dishwasher.

Broiler rack   WB48X47
Broiler pan   WB49X75

Glossary of terms

Appliance Receptacle
Electrical outlet on range backsplash or control panel for plugging in small appliances.

Ballast
Transformer used to set up proper voltage within fluorescent tube lamp.

Calibration
Adjustment of control knob graduations to provide proper range performance.

Circuit
Path of electrical current from power supply through wiring to point of use and back to source.

Circuit Breaker
Device to protect circuit from current overload. "Tripped" circuit breaker interrupts circuit when current exceeds specified amount. See also FUSE.

Circuit Diagram
Drawing using standard symbols to represent path of current flow from power supply through switches and components and back to source. Shows how wiring is connected between components and how internal wiring of components is arranged.

Closed (circuit)
Complete circuit which can conduct electricity.

Cold Pin
Portion of heating unit which extends out from metal sheath and insulation and is welded to the wiring terminal.

Coil
Nickel-chrome alloy resistance wire which heats when current is passed through it. Component of heating unit. See also HEATING UNIT, SHEATH.

Component
Electrically operated part such as a switch, thermostat, etc.

Contact
Switch component which opens and closes to complete or break an electrical circuit.

Continuity
Ability of completed circuit to conduct electricity.

Defective
In this manual, used to mean a component which does not function properly and which must be replaced.

Energize
To supply electrical current for operation of a component.

Feedback
In testing for continuity, current returning to meter through a part of circuit other than component being tested, giving false reading.

Fluorescent Lamp
Chemically-coated, gas-filled tube which uses a complex electrical process to transform ultraviolet energy into visible light.

Fuse
Device to protect circuit from current overload. "Blown" fuse automatically interrupts circuit when current exceeds specified amount. See also CIRCUIT BREAKER, RANGE FUSE.

Fuse Block
Separate part of distribution panel containing large fuses used for electric range circuit. Usually two cartridge-type fuses joined at the handle.

Gasket
Flexible heat-resistant material designed to provide seal and control air flow into oven. Oven gasket may be mounted on front of range body or on the inside of oven door.

Ground
Connection to the earth or to another conducting body which transmits current to the earth. Metal components in a circuit must be grounded to prevent their accidentally becoming electrically charged, causing short circuit or injury.

Heating Unit
Nickel-chrome alloy resistance coil encased in electrical insulation material and steel sheath; generates heat when current is passed through it. Used as range surface unit, and oven bake and broil units.

Inoperative
In this manual, used to mean a component which does not function, but which can be checked and possibly repaired.

Lead
Portion of electrical wiring attached to component.

Nutdriver
Tool used to remove and reinstall hexagonal-head screws or nuts. Resembles a screwdriver with a small socket at the end instead of a blade.

Ohm
Measurement unit for electrical resistance.

Ohmmeter
Battery operated device for determining continuity of a circuit and measuring its resistance.

Open (circuit)
Incomplete circuit which cannot conduct electricity.

Printed Circuit Board (P.C. board)
Solid-state component of self-cleaning oven's temperature control system.

Range Fuse
Device to prevent overload on separate 120-volt circuit within the range which serves appliance receptacle. Automatically interrupts circuit if plugged-in appliance causes excessive power flow.

Resistance
Restriction of current flow in an electrical circuit.

Sheath
Steel protective covering for nickel-chrome alloy resistance coil in heating unit.

Short Circuit
Accidentally created circuit between hot wire and any ground, allowing excessive current flow with little or no resistance.

Solid State
Electrical components incorporating resistors, transistors, etc. Requires no moving parts or mechanical components.

Switch
Device to turn on and off current flow in an electrical circuit.

Terminal
Connection point between wiring and electrical components. Commonly used terminals in ranges are push-on terminals, which are held in place by their snug fit, and eyelet terminals, which consist of a metal ring or bare wire held in position by a terminal screw.

Test Probes
Metal components of ohmmeter which are attached to either end of a circuit during testing for continuity or resistance. See also OHMMETER.

Thermostat
Device for controlling temperature levels in heating unit. Activated by a heat-sensing component.

Transformer
Device for raising or lowering voltage.

Upscale
Reading from ohmmeter that indicates continuity in a circuit.

Volt
Measurement unit for electrical pressure.

Watt
Measurement unit for electrical power.

Index

Index (cont.)

Index (cont.)

Thermostat
adjusting 64
capillary tube
  (high temperature limit) 79
  (dual range) 87
  (non-self-cleaning) 66
non-self-cleaning range 65
oven 64
self-clean dual range 87
self-clean solid-state 81
Timer(see Clock Timer)
Tools
tools and testing equipment 94
Transformer
self-clean oven 77
Sensi-Temp™ surface unit 43, 44

Vent
oven vent 45
Volt-Ohmmeter (VOM) (see
Testing Equipment)

Wall Ovens
accessing 22
description 7
Wiring
"Repairing wiring and
connections" Procedure 5 (p.25)
appliance wire ratings 25
eyelet terminals 26
inspection 25
push-on terminals 26
soldering 26
splicing 26
U-shape terminals 26
wire mountings 25